DAVID
Beckham
my story

DAVID Beckham
my story

as told to
Neil Harman

First published in Great Britain in 1998 by Manchester United Books
an imprint of André Deutsch Ltd

76 Dean Street

London W1V 5HA

Web site: www.vci.co.uk

André Deutsch Ltd is a VCI plc company

Text Copyright © David Beckham 1998

Printed and bound by Butler and Tanner, Frome and London

A catalogue record for this book is available from the British Library

ISBN 0 233 99148 4

Design by Design/Section

CONTENTS

Foreword by Bryan Robson

Afterword by Alessandro Del Piero

Foreword by **Bryan**
Robson

David Beckham is a smashing kid, that should be said straightaway. He is not only a credit to himself, but to his parents and the rest of his family too. A lot of professional footballers out there could do a lot worse than see how David handles himself and try to emulate it.

From the first day he came to Manchester United I remember him as a well-mannered lad who would do anything for you. He seemed to be United daft – he knew all about the club, he was fascinated by it, and I had a suspicion even then that he would turn out to be one of its finest young players. I could sense it.

When I watched the youngsters training, he would be one of the first out there and the last to leave – the kind of dedication you need to succeed as a player and, speaking now as a manager, an attitude you want to see in your players all the time. He pinpointed the weaknesses in his overall game. He wasn't a great tackler, he wasn't especially big, but he worked and worked at it.

When you see those free-kicks he puts away in the Premier League with such incredible power and precision, it is no fluke. I can picture him now at the Cliff training ground – where so much of the groundwork has been put into United's successes over the years – working for ages on striking the ball just right, perfecting his technique, until he was happy he'd got it right.

He scored the kind of goals we see in the Premiership now for United at all levels of youth football. When you are part of a club like Manchester United people are always looking at you, scrutinising everything you do with more intensity than anywhere else in the country. A certain standard is expected and woe betide anyone if they fall beneath it.

I know that certain people like nothing better than to find something to criticise, you are never going to be good enough for some of them, so I can feel for

David when I see how much he has to put up with, but he appears to cope with it all very well. If he was big-headed, the people at the club would soon bring him back down to earth anyway, there's no fear at United of anyone becoming grander than they should be. I see no signs of that with Beckham. Good for him.

It is important to handle yourself well. I was at a dinner earlier this year for United's long-serving youth team coach Eric Harrison, the most successful worker with the young since Jimmy Murphy in the fifties under Matt Busby. I had a couple of minutes in David Beckham's company, and he was telling me about his family, about Victoria, how hard it is sometimes on all of them sometimes. He said how much he was looking forward to becoming a part of Victoria's family. That's smashing.

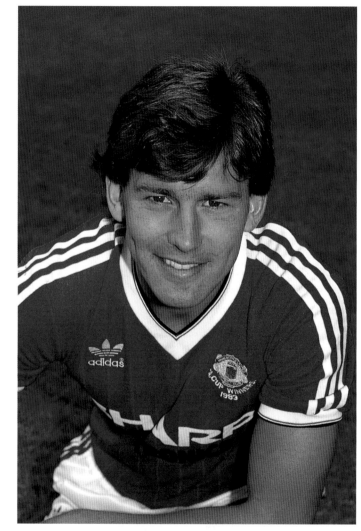

I think people sometimes forget how young these lads are, because they seem to have been around so long. Ryan Giggs is 24, and he's almost a veteran in the United first team; David is 23, and he's a regular at Old Trafford and in the England team. But I'm not surprised at how easily he has handled the transition from club to international football.

When you have his qualities – a lovely touch on the ball and great passing skills – you've got a chance, but he's worked on his stamina as well, which is vital when you play at international level. The fitness of these guys is phenomenal and you have to match them. He's doing that.

You also need to have strong mental resolve, because the expectations on United players are so immense. If you are short of personal character,

United will find it out. I think just being a player for such a magnificent club means you grow up very quickly. The ones who will succeed are those who can identify the best bits of a senior player's make up; but not only that, they spot the worst bits as well, and learn to put the wrong stuff on one side and use the best to their own advantage.

We all make mistakes on the way up, but it is the best players who can see weaknesses in others and make certain they never fail in the same way. The eyes are opened much quicker at Old Trafford. I am sure that David would be the first to admit what an influence Alex Ferguson has been on his career, as he was on mine. Alex has such a paternal feeling towards his young players and I know how much he admires the way David is going about his career and his life. If the young man ever needs a word, he should know that the manager's door is always open.

I'm told that I was David's hero once, that's always nice to know. If I have done anything that can inspire a young player I'm delighted, though it does make me feel a little old! The no.7 shirt at Manchester United was magic for me, and I'm sure it is for David as well.

He is a young player in the finest tradition of Manchester United, he has so much going for him, and I'm thrilled to have this opportunity of expressing a few thoughts on his behalf. If he has half the career I had at Old Trafford, he's going to experience something really special. I think it's fair to say it gives me as much pleasure watching him as he says he had watching me.

I wish him well, as I would wish any United player well.

Bryan Robson
ex-captain of Manchester United and England.
Manager, Middlesbrough F.C.

The Beginning

I was ten years old when they first called me a Little Devil, and, to tell you the truth, that's all I've ever wanted to be. The publicity people say that I was an ordinary kid who went to an ordinary school, and that's right. I wasn't a great scholar, I'll admit to that. There were to be no academic qualifications for me. I wasn't one of those who revelled in schoolwork, indeed, I came away from school on most afternoons with a football under my arm, wondering when the next kick-about would start. In that, I don't suppose I was any different from most of the kids at Chase Lane Junior or, later, Chingford High.

My parents might have wanted me to concentrate better on my

My first picture in the paper came after winning the Fyfield five-a-side tournament.

schoolwork, my Mum often chided me on my reports, but they both knew that I wanted to be a footballer and, with a little bit of luck, that I had the talent to make

it. I never had any pretensions to be a celebrity, and when I think back over the last ten years, it's all been pretty amazing stuff. All of my dreams, well almost all of them, fulfilled, and a lot more to come. Could there be a young man of 23 with more to look forward to?

It's easy to say it now, but all I ever wanted to do was play football for Manchester United. The dream has come true. There was never another team for me. From the first time my dad took me to see them play at White Hart Lane and I watched the likes of Bryan Robson, Gordon Strachan,

Frank Stapleton and Remi Moses in those wonderful red shirts, there were stars in my eyes and the club had taken a hold over me. That fascination remains today and, I hope, it will for the rest of my career.

You can never tell what's going to happen in football, so I don't like to try to speculate on what might or might not occur in the future, but at this point in time, there's no desire on my part to play football for anybody else.

I suppose it's all my dad's fault. Although I was brought up in Chingford with White Hart Lane not that far away to the west down the North Circular, and West Ham the other way, my dad Ted was a United supporter. Always. He edged me – ever so subtly – towards playing for United, but he didn't have to push too hard. The moment I saw Bryan Robson in the no.7 shirt, I wanted to be like him, playing in so many colossal games in the biggest stadiums in the world, and to wear the same shirt. You cannot believe how proud it makes me to be United's no.7, following in the footsteps of Robbo and, later, the remarkable Eric Cantona.

It seems a mighty long way from Ridgeway Rovers under-8s, but that's where the dream began, as a scrawny kid with a lot of my schoolmates, wanting to score goals, to be as famous as those we saw on the television each week. I wanted to be all the stars rolled into one. The playing fields of the East End of London were my Old Trafford. My first picture in the local paper (there have been a few more taken of me since then, and not always in the manner I would have wished) came the day when my local side won the Fyfield five-

a-side soccer tournament. I remember a later match we won 23-0 in the under-10s against St Andrew's, and you could imagine how proud I was to see the report saying that David Beckham had played an outstanding game on the right wing. Shades of things to come, I'd like to think. My grandad has kept a meticulous record of all my newspaper cuttings, from the very first day and I'm thankful to him for that, because I'll always have them to look back on and cherish. From the very start, people have written nice things about me – though to be labelled 'Chingford football sensation' at 12 is a little bit cringe-making.

My father has been the greatest influence on my career, I'm sure even Alex Ferguson wouldn't mind too much me saying that. Dad had had trials with a couple of amateur clubs when he was a teenager, but it hadn't worked out the way he would have liked. He says he's had more of a kick out of watching me play and progress than he ever did out of playing the game himself, and if I've helped make him proud of me, then that is all a son could want. I know the sacrifices he has made for me to succeed and it's only right that I give him reason to enjoy watching my career blossom.

When I wanted someone to kick a ball around with back in those days of dreaming, Dad was there, sometimes until it was so dark we could hardly see each other. Mum would be worried, because it would be 11 o'clock at night and we still weren't home from one of Dad's Sunday League matches, but it was only because I still hadn't practised my corners enough and I was begging him to stay on and be in goal for a few more.

When I needed to be somewhere for a trial, a match, or anything else connected with the game, Dad was there to make certain I made it in time. When I wanted advice, he was there, although in the end he would always say 'It's up to you David, you do what you think is best for yourself. I'll give you all the advice you want, but you have to decide what you want to do.'

With that kind of support behind me from the outset, I have learnt to stand on my own two feet and not be afraid to make the choices that have been beneficial for my career. It is important to know what you believe is best and not be afraid to go for it.

Dad implanted so many of the best practices into me - keep improving, keep practising, keep your love of the game. And sign for Manchester United. I can only begin to guess at how much pleasure it gives my dad, and my mum too, of course, to see me in the United first team, and representing my country. They never miss a game. They have always been there for me, supportive and loving. Everything I ever achieve in the game will be down to their encouragement.

My parents never doubted me for a minute, and in my own innocent way, I never doubted myself either.

CHAPTER 1

I suppose the real breakthrough came when I was about 11 years old and home from school one afternoon – there mustn't have been any football practice that day – watching Blue Peter on BBC1. They ran a feature on the Bobby Charlton Soccer Coaching School. There were going to be skills sessions across the country and the winners from the regions would have the chance to compete in the final at Old Trafford. Old Trafford – could you believe it? I raced into the kitchen and asked my Mum whether I could go in for it and she said yes, of course I could. My grandad (a Tottenham fan through and through, even now I can't get him to change his allegiance) said he would pay the £125 it cost for me to take part. How ever can I thank him enough? It turned out to be the defining moment in my career.

I qualified for the final by winning the London area competition, where there seemed to be hundreds of kids. We were broken up into small groups, and had to impress the judges with our control of the ball using

different parts of the body: the head, chest and feet. There were dribbling skills, passing skills, short passing and ball juggling. All those practice sessions in the pitch-black with my Dad paid off.

The final was at Old Trafford and I stayed in the Halls of Residence in Manchester. As I was a little homesick I made up something about having a toothache to get a bit of sympathy. I remember my parents drove up, stayed with some relatives nearby and asked if I wanted to go home. Of course, I didn't want to really. Even so, I was so nervous on the night before the final at Old Trafford, I couldn't eat. Some of the elements of the competition were done away from the public eye, but when they took us

Everything I have done in football, I owe to my Mum and Dad.

out onto the pitch for the last two series, the dribbling and the passing, I thought my legs were going to turn to jelly. The United first team was out there in the middle warming up for the game against Tottenham (we were at the end where I was to score my first goal for the club eight years later). It's pretty common knowledge now that I scored 1106 points, which was the highest ever and for that, I won a trip to Barcelona.

Somewhere in the back of my mind, I remember Sir Bobby Charlton saying that I was the best 11 year old he'd seen in six years of the school. You can imagine how fantastic that made me feel. Halfway through the final part of the competition, someone came up to me and

Sir Bobby Charlton said I was the best 11 year old he'd seen in six years running his school.

told me that I'd won, and they announced over the loudspeaker that the winner was David Beckham ... from Essex. The Tottenham fans started to chant 'Yiddo, Yiddo', thinking I was one of them.

**A United shirt,
a United ball,
a United-crazy kid.**

Then it was announced that I was a United fan, and the Tottenham followers started to boo me. Jeered for the first time in my life, and at Old Trafford of all places.

Still they are magic memories, as are those from the trip to Barcelona, where I met Mark Hughes, Gary Lineker and the club's manager at the time, Terry Venables. Part of the prize was the chance to train with the Barcelona reserve and youth teams, to practise with them and live together in the hostel accommodation they have at the Nou Camp. It was a thrilling time, and although I walked around with my mouth gaping open most of the time, it was an incredible experience, and a great introduction to the professional way of life.

At home, they were calling me The Kid with the Golden Boots. Pretty strong stuff for an 11 year old. Halfway through the trip to Spain, I had to come home because my club, Ridgeway Rovers, were playing in the Waltham Forest under-12 Cup Final at White Hart Lane and I couldn't possibly have missed that. I took the flight on my own, which didn't upset me half as much as the fact that we lost 2-1 and I didn't have a very good match. My parents took me back to the airport for the second week in Spain, and although I was really upset to go back without a winner's medal, the rest of the trip was a real eye-opener. They took us to one of the matches at the stadium, which was a fabulous experience. I could hardly have expected to be back there as part of the United squad for a European Cup tie.

Soon after that, my life really changed, and for once in his life, my Dad missed the game. I was playing on the right wing for Waltham Forest under-12s against Redbridge, and it was one of my best games for the district (so my Mum said). I was the last boy out of the changing rooms afterwards – a habit I haven't grown

Two weeks in Barcelona was the prize ... Who's that with David Beckham?

out of – when my Mum called me over. I could tell there was a different kind of excitement in her voice when she said, 'it's lucky you had a good game today', and I asked her why. 'Because there was a scout from Manchester United watching and he's going to call your Dad later about coming round to the house tonight and discuss taking you to the club for trials.' Apparently, I was so overcome, I leapt in the air and then started to cry. I had wondered if United had forgotten about me since the Bobby Charlton competition, because I was so far away from the club living in London and I didn't know anything about the scouting systems that

professional clubs employ. As far as a young lad was concerned, Manchester might have been the other side of the world. That day I knew they hadn't forgotten me.

Malcolm Fidgeon was United's scout in the London area, and he used to come to the house at 8 o'clock in the morning to drive me up to Old Trafford for the trials, each one lasting a week. My mum tells me that I stood at the front window and if it got to five past eight, I'd start to get

I couldn't get enough of United as a kid. I knew it was the club for me.

really nervous and wonder if he was ever going to come. Then I would see his car, dash upstairs, grab my kit from the top of the bed, say a quick 'bye' over my shoulder and off we went up the motorway. Those were brilliant days.

When United's first team were playing in London, we used to go and watch them as often as we could. It made for some amusing incidents. Mum thinks of everything, so when she knew we were going to meet Alex Ferguson for the first time, she had a pen neatly wrapped for me to present to him. I remember he said it was the pen he was going to use to sign me with.

That meeting was at the West Lodge Park where United were staying before a match in London. Although I had been to the club for trials but, I realise now, that they never wasted an opportunity to try to make an impression on a budding young player. I can't remember where United were playing the next day, I was so excited to be invited to meet some of the players I regarded as heroes. The manager was there with Archie Knox, who was his assistant then. I sat down, looked at the menu, and ordered salmon steak, thinking it was a normal steak. Up came this huge piece of fish, and I didn't know what to do. I was afraid to send it back, in case the manager thought I didn't know what I was doing. I ate it, but I'll never forget the look on Archie Knox's face. This spindly lad devouring this great big piece of fish. What did we have here?

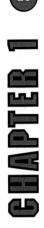

CHAPTER 1

The next time United were in London, I was their mascot for the game at Upton Park. I turned up in my best suit and a Manchester United tie, of course, and then got changed into my red and white kit for the two-minute warm up with players like the captain Steve Bruce and Bryan Robson. There was all the usual stuff, shaking hands with the referee, the opposing captain – Billy Bonds, I think – and then it was back into my suit for the match. I managed to sneak my way into the row behind the United bench to watch the game. When Clayton Blackmore was brought on and the TV cameras showed a close-up of the substitution, there was this young kid with spiky hair right in the picture. My first TV exposure standing right behind Alex Ferguson as he shouted out his instructions. I was learning at his shoulder even then. Wide eyed and innocent maybe, but I was taking it all in. Even then, I couldn't get enough of United. I knew it was the club for me.

Actually, the choice for me in the end was either Tottenham or Manchester United. There was only one choice really, but Tottenham had made an offer, so I had to take it seriously. My Dad sat me down, he didn't put any pressure on me; he just said that I had to make up my mind and he would stand by me either way. I think he knew which way I was going to decide, so he was on pretty safe ground. He did say that whoever I decided to join, he would be there for me, there were no problems with that.

I don't know how many parents would have the kind of faith in their child that lets him make his mind up for himself.

Prior to the offer I used to spend all my six-week summer holidays at United. I used to just love being around the place, even if there wasn't any training to get involved in. I so wanted to be a part of it. I think they thought I was a bit of a pest, because I'd either be down at Littleton Road, where United had a couple of training pitches, or at the Cliff. Every day.

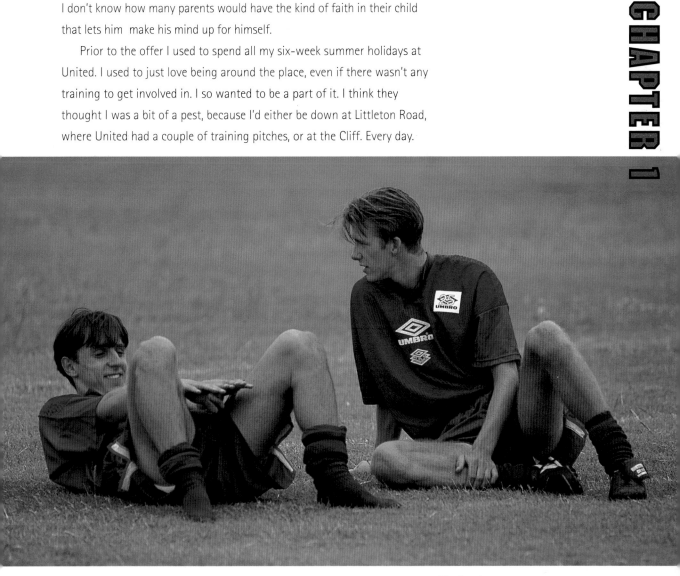

There were trials going on through the week and I didn't want to miss a moment. I was in love with the place. I still am.

So it was the end of collecting glasses at Walthamstow Dog Track, earning a few pence for every one I managed to grab from under the noses of the punters. I had loved my nights there, it was great pocket money, but it was time for me to leave London behind and head for Manchester. United beckoned and I wanted to be there, in the famous red shirt. I didn't think that anything could stop me.

I suppose when I first signed for United at 16, I sometimes wondered if I would make it. In spite of my confidence there was the nagging

Early days at Manchester United.

thought that it might all end after two years and how would I ever be able to tell my mates that I was being sent home from the club of my dreams? Even after all that has happened, my mates still regard me as a mate. They come and stay with me if they have the time, which is the way it should be. They don't treat me any differently and I would hate it if they did. I'm still the same David Beckham I always was, and that's the way I want it to stay, whatever others might want to think or say about me.

Moving to Manchester meant leaving home, but I'd got used to being away, so it wasn't that difficult. I recall that my first digs as a 16 year old were just off the Bury New Road but I'd moved within a year. My third 'home' in Manchester was the one that holds the greatest affection. It was the home in Lower Broughton of the terrific Annie and Tony Kay, where I stayed for three years. Mark Hughes, a legend in my eyes, stayed in the room that I had for a number of years.

The family are United through and through. I think Annie has been a landlady for as long as I've been alive, so she's seen some comings and goings in her time. It was just like being an addition to their own family, they looked after me brilliantly, and the great thing, especially for a teenager, was that they allowed me to have my space. I owe them a lot.

I felt as though I could always tell my troubles (there weren't that many!) to Annie. You need to be happy where you're living if you want to be playing your best, and these digs were perfect.

Relaxing away from the training ground (above). Playing for the Manchester United Youth Team (left).

The house is only about 100 yards from the entrance to the Cliff, but I have to confess, even though I was in my teens and an apprentice professional footballer, I can't remember walking to the training ground from the moment I passed my test onwards. I always drove. I suppose it was because I felt my cars – my pride and joy – were safe at the ground, locked away with the security we have to have with so many people coming and going.

My first car was an Escort, then I bought myself a brand new Volkswagen Golf, then I had a Honda Prelude which was a club car; my fourth was an M3 Convertible and my fifth is the Porsche. I like changing cars, and I suppose if I can afford to do it, I'll keep doing it. It isn't a crime to have a nice car.

In my first year as a fully-fledged youth team player, I actually didn't get many games. Nobby Stiles was in charge of the B team at that time, and when I graduated to the A team, which was managed by Eric Harrison, I still wasn't a regular. In fact, I didn't play in any of the rounds of the 1992 FA Youth Cup until we reached the semi-final second leg against Tottenham at White Hart Lane. I was called into the side and I thought I played well. We reached the final in which we beat Crystal Palace over two legs. I scored at Selhurst Park, at the same end where, five years later, I was to score one of the goals of my life. It was my first trophy and first winner's

Manchester United make you feel part of a very big family. We all get on, there are no rows, no bickering, but we all want to make it. Kevin Pilkington, me, Phil Neville, Simon Davies and Chris Casper have a lark.

medal with United. The first of many, it was to turn out.

I suppose it was in my second spell as a regular in the youth team that I first started to notice people writing things about me, especially in the local *Manchester Evening News* because that was always lying around on the kitchen table in Annie and Tony's house. We used to pick it up to see if we got a mention. I didn't take too much notice about what people were saying about me, though most of it was pretty complimentary. Like all of us in the squad, it was a matter of buckling down, working hard, doing what you were told and not listening to anyone but the people that mattered, the coaching staff and your family.

Eric Harrison was a great influence on my career. He had been at United as youth coach for years and I think it just goes to prove that there are certain people who are cut out to handle the young players. Eric was a constant source of inspiration, but he could give you a hard time if

he wanted to. Even though I've been a first-team player for a couple of years now, I still ring Eric up at home, or we go out for a meal and talk about where my career is going, or if he thinks I should be working harder on anything. It's important to know in football whom you can trust to give you the best advice.

All the young players had respect for Eric, because you knew that what he was telling you was right because he has an understanding of what it is like to try to succeed for Manchester United. He was the guy who told me how important it was to come back in the afternoons and work on my own if I felt there were things in my game that needed attention. He got me into the routine of practising my free-kicks, corners, and long- and short-range passing.

I used to go down to the Cliff in the evenings and do some coaching myself at the School of Excellence, to train with the younger lads, to get involved with them, and try to help them on. I remember in my short time on trial at Tottenham as a kid how, when the older pros used to come along and take part in the coaching, it used to buck you up no end. Actually, Sol Campbell was at White Hart Lane in those coaching sessions, it is unbelievable how our careers have come along and now we're both in the England team.

When your Youth Team is winning tournaments, you know the club's got an exciting future. It's no wonder that Manchester United is the best club in the country.

Alex Ferguson

The manager of Manchester United has probably done more for my career than even I'm aware of. There is a special aura about him that is difficult to explain, but he has a hold over the players at the club and I don't think we'll ever be able to work out what it is. Some managers have a certain magic, Alex Ferguson has it in spades.

He is always with us, each one of us individually, but essentially we are a family, a team that wants to do well for United and we feed off his unbelievable desire for success. It's all he wants, it's all we want as well. I was scared stiff of Alex Ferguson the first time I met him and I still am, I suppose. I was 12 when I took him that pen, he called me David, and my Dad has always said he has never met anyone with such a remarkable memory for every young person's name. United have always prided themselves on their youth policy and that all stems from the manager and his ability to make young kids feel part of the family straight away.

I was in awe of him, of course, but he charmed Mum and Dad, and that charm has never worn off. They think he's a terrific man, someone with whom they would be more than happy to trust their son and that is crucial when it comes to deciding what is best for your future. When you take into account all that he's achieved

for United, the time he spends involved – I never beat him into the training ground even when I lived 100 yards away – the pleasure he gets from bringing young players through and how much time and trouble he takes to be interested and involved in all of their lives, it is no wonder that Manchester United are the best club in the country.

His achievements are well documented – four championships in five seasons, FA Cup triumphs, two doubles, and so many successes further down the playing scale with the A, B and youth teams at United, which count for so much. I believe a lot of the response he gets from his players can be put down to the way he treats us, and what an abiding respect we all hold for him. There's not one player at United who doesn't have some kind of fear of the gaffer, but it's not a dread of him, more a respect for what he stands for. And what he's done for us all.

It is difficult to go into specifics, about how he might have turned a game around, about any pieces of private advice, because that is how

The gaffer and his no.2. Alex Ferguson and Brian Kidd try to get our attention.

they should remain, private. All players go through times when they need someone to turn to, when they need reassurance, and the manager's door is always open.

He gave me my first team debut as a 17 year old in the Coca-Cola Cup at Brighton in October 1992. I came on for Andrei Kanchelskis, with about 20 minutes left. We were leading 1-0 but they equalised. I got a bit of a mouthful at the end. I didn't think I was personally responsible for the result, but I felt like it from the roasting I got from the manager. I think the gist of his message was 'you're in the big time now, son, this is what it's all about.' The way he put his message across brought me right back down to earth.

The manager has a habit of doing that. Have I had the hair-dryer treatment (the famous blast from the manager at close range, face to face, nose to nose almost)? A few times, yes, and one always sticks in my mind, and Gary Neville's. We laugh about it now, but thinking back, it didn't seem so funny at the time. We were both pretty cocky teenagers in the reserves and playing against Everton at Goodison Park we lost 3-0. To be truthful, we were absolutely slaughtered, nothing went right. I can't remember being in a United side that played so badly.

The manager's door is always open, but his face isn't always smiling.

At the end of the game we just want to get changed, get back onto the coach and get home, but the manager suddenly came in, stood a couple of inches from my face and gave me the blast to end all blasts. I was standing there, quivering, hardly knowing where to look. The next day, nothing was mentioned, the point had been made and that was it. I've never known the manager to bear grudges. Once it has been said, it's said, it's over. The manager doesn't let things linger because he knows once the message has been said, it has got through.

In terms of personal advice, of course I've needed it from time to time. There have been things that the manager has done that have upset me. Even made me mad. At the start of the 1997-8 season, he

A big European night to come. The boss speaks to the press.

made it clear that he thought I'd been played too much through the summer, which involved Le Tournoi in France with the England squad, that I was worn out and I wasn't as fresh as I should have been. He left me out of the squad for the Charity Shield match against Chelsea and, instead, told me he was sending me down with the reserves to play against Bournemouth. I wasn't happy about it at all. After all I was 22 years old, and at that age you feel as if you can run forever, especially at the start of a season. I don't know the motives for the manager's decision but I went to Bournemouth and scored one of the best goals of my life. You could say I was a little bit inspired.

Someone told me that in an article the next morning, Tommy Docherty, a former manager of United, had said he thought it

Revelling in another victory for his Reds.

was an insult to leave me out of the side. I'll tell Mr Docherty this, it might have hurt my pride a little bit, there might have been an incentive to do something a bit special, but I have never been insulted playing for Manchester United. It is an honour to pull on the shirt

wherever the manager thinks it best. The gaffer was said to have been enraged when he read such things. I can honestly say that Alex Ferguson has never done anything to me unless it's in my best interest, it just takes a player a little time to understand and appreciate these things.

Anyway, I got the call to join the first team squad back in London, and I was on the bench for the Wembley occasion. I thought I should have played, but every player worth his salt thinks that. The manager has continued to say he would pick me only when he thought it was right. I came on as a substitute in the second half and the press made a lot out of the fact that they had spelt my name incorrectly as 'Beckam' on the back of my shirt.

I didn't say anything about being on the bench to anyone other than my closest family and friends. My Dad told me not to worry about it, he said that when the time was right I would be back in. I believed I should have been playing in every game. I was substitute at Tottenham on the first day of the season and I was not very happy about that. It was Teddy Sheringham's debut for the club after his move from Spurs in the summer and we were drawing

0-0 when the manager brought me on. I was determined to have an impact and from one of my better crosses, Ramon Vega put through an own-goal and we won 2-1.

Yes, I truly believed I had got my own back. Don't think for one minute I had accepted the fact the manager was right. Young players, young England players, young players who want desperately to play, don't want to listen to people telling them to slow down for their

The name is spelt wrong, but who cares? Not Peter Schmeichel obviously.

own good. I wanted to prove to him how important I was to the team, especially with Eric Cantona leaving in the summer. With the arrival of Teddy Sheringham everyone wanted to put a stamp on their place in the first team.

I wasn't happy being a substitute. I hated it. But there I was again, having to warm the bench against Southampton. I came on and scored the winner. I was sub at Wimbledon, and came on and scored twice in a 5-2 victory. I think I made a point. I haven't been substitute very often since.

What makes Alex Ferguson so special? It is his determination, his will to win. It is what he has done, what he's doing now and what he'll continue to do for Manchester United and everybody involved with the club. He has never let me down, and I don't intend to let him down, either. He's the first person at work at seven in the morning, makes his own tea and toast, and he's the last one to leave. A lot of people don't see that, the meticulous manner, the work behind the scenes, the coaching, the keeping tabs on the young players, the amazing memory he has for detail, and his command of tactics.

All that most people see of him is on match days, getting so

intensely involved, looking at his stopwatch, chewing his piece of gum in the dug-out. Or having gum thrown at him from the opposing dug-out as happened when he was aggrieved over that terrible tackle by Feyenoord's Paul Bosvelt on Dennis Irwin in Rotterdam last November.

There are only a certain amount of people you meet in your life who leave a real impression on you, and Alex Ferguson is certainly one of those people. Next to my Dad, he's been the greatest influence on me

and will be, I hope, for many years to come. The manager has seen it all before. He's told me about young players he had at Aberdeen when he was the manager there, who played too much football early in their careers, and who didn't make it into their thirties. Some of them got bad injuries through over-playing, some just couldn't cope with the number of matches that they wanted to play. He can pass that kind of knowledge on when a player doesn't really appreciate why he's been left out.

Of course, I value what he says to me. He has always been supportive and he seems to know what I'm experiencing even before I understand it

With the Charity Shield. Teddy Sheringham picks up his first United medal.

myself sometimes. The manager has pulled me aside a few times, either for a word of encouragement, or if he feels I need a bit of a gee-up. I don't think I've needed many of those. The same is true of Glenn Hoddle, the England coach. When someone like him takes the time to take you to one side, you have to listen.

When I signed my professional forms for Manchester United, it was on my 14th birthday. The club presented me with a huge cake and the manager came along and joined in the chorus of 'Happy Birthday'. It seems a lifetime ago, but it's only been nine years, nine incredibly fulfilling years at Old Trafford. Of course there have been ups and down, they are a part of life. It would be strange if people agreed with everything that has been done to them by others who affect their lives. But there has never been any doubt who's in charge and what he means to the success of the club.

Life is a beach . . . The gaffer and Kiddo get the lads in shape in pre-season training.

A spell at
Preston

At Manchester United you are treated as someone special, and that's a wonderful thing for a young lad trying to make his way in the game. The facilities are superb, they find you the best digs and the banter between the young boys is smashing. But we all know we're fighting to get into the best team in the country. There are ups and downs along the way. I suppose one of the most worrying moments for me was when the manager called me in and told me that Preston North End had been on the phone, asking if they could take me on a month's loan and that he had agreed.

What was an impressionable 19 year old supposed to think about that? I was shocked at first, then a little hurt that he should want to let me go. Then I was downright worried about it. What if United didn't fancy me any more? I asked my dad what I should do and he said straight away to go, and put my heart and soul into it. If a club of the calibre of Preston had come along and was willing to take you for a month, the least you could do was show them the same respect in return, and give them everything you've got. I was in United's reserves at the time, and although there were a lot of good players in the side, it was nothing like playing in the Football League for a club like Preston. There was a lot more experience to be gained from playing out there. I have to say that I didn't exactly relish the idea straight away, but after a couple of sessions with the Preston lads, they had made me feel right at home. The manager, Gary Peters, took me out into the middle of the training pitch right away and said 'Right, this fella is going to take all the free-kick and all the corners, because he's much better at it than any of you lot.' I didn't know where to look, but the lads took it all in good heart.

I suppose a lot of them might have thought I'd be there giving it the big-time Charlie stuff, but I think they realised I was taking it very seriously.

It was the first time in my career that I felt I had a couple of points to prove.

I needed to know that I had the ability to survive and play in a league where I was probably going to get lumps kicked out of me, and I was prepared to put my reputation as one of Manchester United's young 'stars' on the line. I wanted to be a professional footballer for United, and if it meant suffering in someone else's cause, then I'd do it. It didn't matter to me what the personal sacrifice was.

It was important too, that I showed Preston how much respect I had for them. I could have stayed in Manchester, driven to Deepdale on Fridays, trained the day before the match and then played, but that wouldn't have been right. If I was in this, as my Dad said, I was in it 100 per cent. I drove from my digs every morning (I'd just bought myself a brand new Golf at 19 years of age, so I suppose I couldn't have blamed them for thinking I was a bit big-time) and enjoyed every minute of it. I was sub for the first game, came on

and did well. I scored from a free-kick in my second for the winner and then direct from a corner in my third game. I was man-of-the-match three times in my four games for them and no one begrudged me a moment of that personal success.

I was one of the team, and that was the way I wanted it. This wasn't some sort of glory trip, I wanted to be part of the team, part of the club, it was very important to me to be accepted. To be honest, I would have stayed another month if they'd wanted me to, but Alex Ferguson called me back because he was a bit short of players, and I actually made my first-team debut in the Premier League for United on the following weekend at Leeds in a goalless draw. I'm not sure I would have been as well prepared for a game like that coming straight up from the reserves as I was having been playing League football for Preston. It was a very valuable month for me, giving me useful experience and opening my eyes to what football was like somewhere other than Manchester United. To be honest, I suppose we are pampered at United, everything is done to make sure we're on the ball all the time. You are treated as something special, even when you're playing for the youth team or the reserves. When I turned up on the first day at Preston, I remember being given this pretty old training kit and at the end of the session I threw it into the middle of the dressing room, expecting someone to pick it up and have it cleaned for me for the next morning. But I was told I had to take it home and wash it myself (fortunately the landlady washed it for me). I would say that the month at Preston turned my career around, setting everything off. I needed to be picked up a little bit, to be encouraged, and Preston did that for me.

I don't get back there as often as I should, and I was really sorry to see that Gary Peters lost his job – he is a smashing bloke, and a very good manager. I met Tom Finney, now Sir Tom, a couple of times. What a very nice man. Extremely polite. He came over and met me when I first joined, and told me a little bit about Preston and said he hoped I would enjoy the experience of playing there. I didn't have the pleasure of seeing Tom Finney play, of course, but I've been told so much about him, and clearly he is one of the greatest players ever to wear an England shirt. If I finish my career with as many people saying as many nice things about me as they do about Sir Tom, I shouldn't have anything to be worried about.

Striking a pose in the England shirt that means so much to me.

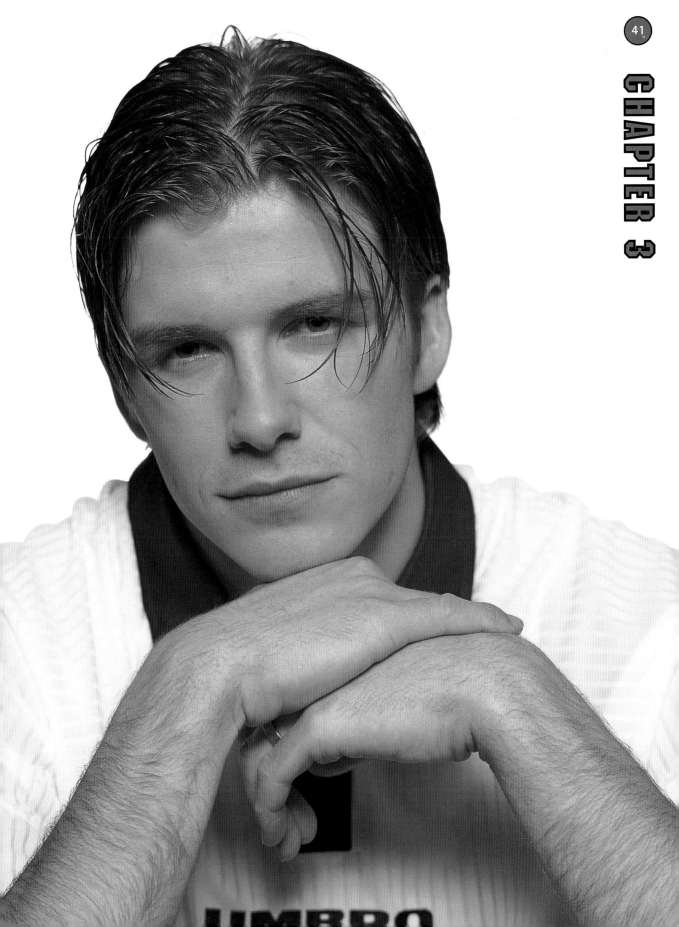

CHAPTER 4

Dealing with the Media

All that newspapers used to mean to me were all those cuttings in the scrapbooks my grandad has kept meticulously for so many years, and the papers that my dad buys every day, cutting out and filing the articles written about David Beckham, the footballer. I have grown to realise in recent times, that the Press means an awful lot more than that. It is not always easy to put up with the other side of the operation.

I love to see my name in the paper, on the back pages, who wouldn't? Now though, when things are written about me, good or bad, on the footballing front, I find out from my family, because I don't buy the papers myself any more.

The football coverage in England is, in many cases, very good indeed, even though the popular end of the market wants to bring you crashing down the minute they have built you up. I just want to play football, live my life to the full, and not be hammered every time I step a tiny bit out of line. When the media intrudes into your private life and

makes you have to change the way you want to live, I think the Press has gone too far.

I suppose you will have noticed that I have a fiancée: Victoria. She has become one of the most famous young women in the world. We are deeply in love.

There was nothing particularly romantic about our first meeting.

We don't get that much time to spend with each other, so when we do, we tend to do everything together.

Victoria came to watch me play for Manchester United at Old Trafford one afternoon and said she wanted to meet for a drink afterwards. We decided to travel down to London on the Sunday,

and from then on, we've been inseparable. I couldn't believe that we'd passed each other before in the players' lounge at Chelsea. At first I didn't know she was in there, but when I found out that she was, I was too shy to approach her. I just waved at her, not exactly the most romantic gesture ever.

Then I asked those who knew her where she used to spend her evenings and I travelled down to London on the off chance I might bump into her at this particular rendezvous, but she wasn't there. Another opportunity lost. But one afternoon, when we were in the dressing room at Old Trafford before a game against Sheffield Wednesday, the manager happened to say that a couple of the Spice Girls were coming to the game. Apparently, or so Gary Neville says, before I knew it, I was up on my feet asking 'Which ones?'

When I went into the lounge after the game, Victoria was there with Mel C. We started to talk and arranged a meeting, hoping to keep it as quiet as we could. It wasn't easy. We had to disguise ourselves when we went out – collar pulled up, baseball caps pulled down, that sort of thing – which is another reason why we find the Press interest suffocating at times.

The relationship hasn't been made easier by the Press. We're very young to have to endure the kind of coverage we're getting, but we'll see it through. From the word go, people were following us about. There was a photographer permanently stationed outside my house near Manchester for weeks. When I left for training he was there, following me on his motorcycle, and then he tailed me home afterwards. I half-expected him to be there every time I went to the toilet. I made the police aware of what was happening, and they told me they would keep an eye on the situation.

These kind of things can be scary, and we try not to get too worried about them, but it's not always easy.

I don't know what it is about people that they want to start finding fault so much of the time. I represent England at football and I'm proud to do it. I think there should be more praise given to those who have earned such an opportunity, rather than trying to pick bits out of them.

When the media found out I was going out with Victoria, they started to write pieces that were supposed to be based on stories from my mates and former girlfriends of mine. All of it was total nonsense.

I don't want to be the in papers for anything other than for my football. Some people might find that hard to believe, but it's true. Over Christmas, Victoria and I were all over the front pages – surely there are more important things happening in the world than two families having a Christmas lunch and Victoria and I taking our dogs for walk.

We thought we did brilliantly to keep our relationship secret for as long as we did. We've been together now for over a year, so there's no

doubt in our minds that we'll stay together. The announcement of our engagement wasn't something we had meticulously planned, it just happened because we felt the timing was right. We aren't getting married until 1999, so there is plenty to look forward to. Perhaps now that we have got the announcement over and done with, we can concentrate on our lives until the big day approaches.

It will be a momentous day for both of us. It will be great fun, but there is a serious side to it as well, because that is the way it should be when you're getting married. I couldn't be any happier than I am today. It is not everyone who is able to enjoy what he always dreamed of doing, and then find his dream woman who says 'Yes' when he proposes to her. I guess I'm a pretty lucky young man.

I couldn't be luckier – finding my dream woman and then she said 'yes' when I proposed!

Obviously the Press interest will die down a little bit, now that people realise it's serious and we just want to be happy. I'm sure newspaper readers are fed up to the back teeth with seeing our faces in front of them every morning. Just as we are tired of being there. I don't see the news value in two people coming out of a restaurant. I'm amazed really that the media finds my personal life so interesting.

Victoria has a lovely smile, and not a lot of people see it, because of the image she has to portray as Posh Spice. She's my best friend and that's one of the main reasons we get on so well together. We can talk to each other, we understand and appreciate the pressures we both face (and yes, I think their music is great). It can be difficult to cope, but I would never change my personality. Why should I?

It is infuriating sometimes when people who don't know me, make a judgement about me because I drive around in smart cars and wear the latest designer clothes. They have never met me, or spoken to me, so what gives them the right to say what I'm like? Ask anyone who knows me well, and they'll tell you that I'm just an ordinary lad who happens to have a talent for which I'm well paid. I'm lucky, I understand that, but it doesn't make me anything special.

To tell you the truth, I'd rather stay in on my own at night if no one is up to see me. I'm not a party animal, I never have been. If Victoria isn't in town, or my friends and family aren't up to visit, I'm more than happy with my own company. I've got a stack of videos at home, mostly football and yes, they're mostly of Manchester United. I tape *Match of the Day* every weekend, and I'm currently hooked on the American comedy *Friends*, which is fantastic, the best new show in years.

A night in front of the television on your own might not be everyone's idea of a good time, but that's one of the downsides of being who I am with the profile I have. I can't go out too much, because there are people out there who are just waiting to trap someone like me.

CHAPTER 4

Not exactly dressed for the Open, but relaxing at the golf range. Looks as though I caught that one pretty well.

Probably because I've been away from home for so long, I'm happy with my own company. I'll go for a meal on my own, probably to the local Chinese. They put me at a table in a corner and no one bothers me.

It's terrible when you consider that I rarely draw my curtains at home, simply because I don't want people coming up to see who or what is inside. Even so, it's very hard to escape it all. Victoria and I have tried a couple of different places to get away from all the attention. Sometimes we haven't been seen or hassled and those are the best times of all. Sadly, it doesn't always work out that way.

We thought we were bound to be undiscovered when we went to St Tropez for a short break last year. We'd just got there, and decided to go for a walk along the beach, thinking we'd have some peace and quiet for ourselves. It was unbelievable, we didn't even see the photographer. The next day there were pictures all over the papers. It is hard to find any privacy.

Has it affected me as a player? Well, the remarks from supporters have become a little bit choice, and at times they've been totally over the top. The manager has told me to try to forget about them, to concentrate on my own game, but it's not always that easy. It started in the final game of last season at West Ham, with some very vicious things being said, and I couldn't believe it when I was warming up behind the goal at Wembley for this year's Charity Shield, and the chant started up again. My reaction, to put my hand behind one of my ears as if I couldn't hear what they were saying, was a spontaneous gesture. Some people said I was right to react in the way I did, others thought I'd played into the barrackers' hands.

Maybe I should just have ignored it, but it's hard not to react to those kind of comments if they are being chanted about someone you love. I seem to hear it everywhere now, it's become a bit monotonous. I suppose they think they're upsetting me, but they aren't, not any more. I suppose, when it comes down to it, they're envious. I read an article in an Italian magazine about me and Victoria and I thought it was very revealing. There are plenty of Italian footballers who have famous wives and girlfriends, and I'm certain there are plenty of Italian people who could find reason to have a go at them because of it, but there's nothing like the kind of stick I've had to put up with.

It does seem a strangely English attitude towards people who are

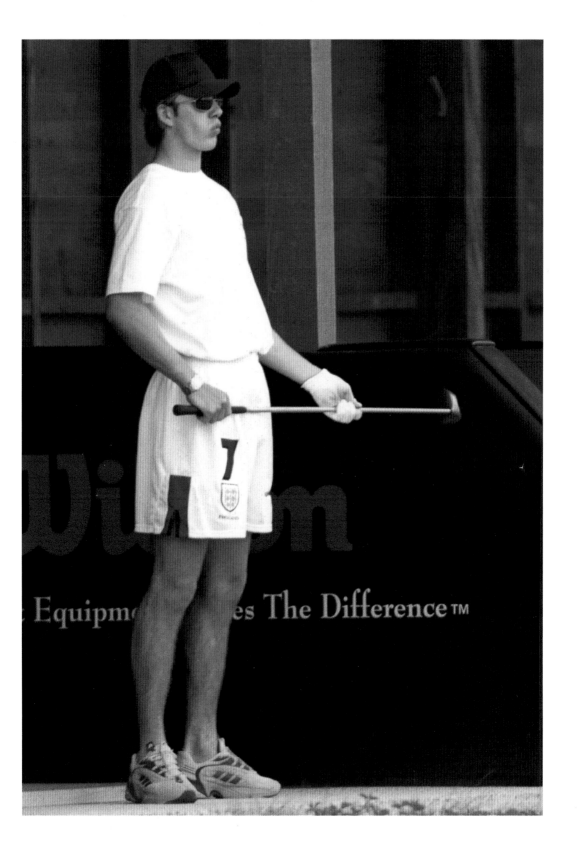

thought to be successful, or different, call it what you like. I've been accused of becoming more aggressive this season, especially after the Feyenoord tie in the Champions' League at Old Trafford when I was fortunate to get away with one tackle the media picked up on. I think I've always had a bit of aggression in my make-up, you need it to succeed. I was often told that I was too small when I was a kid, I remember that the people involved with the England Schoolboys set-up reckoned I'd never make it as a pro because I was so slight. The Essex under-15 coach Martin Heather was outraged when he heard what the England people were saying about me. I remember him jokingly telling my dad that to get into the under-15 side you needed sideburns, two children and a car. It makes you wonder how many other talented players have fallen by the wayside because they weren't built like Desperate Dan.

But back to the aggression. There was one game, against Bolton, when the United players realised that the barracking was worse than it had ever been, and noticed that it was affecting me more than it had before. I remember Gary Neville, my best friend in football, coming over to

ask me if I was all right. I said I was fine, but I just couldn't let it go over my head without reacting. I did put myself about a bit that day, because of what their fans were shouting. The manager got me into his office the next morning, about 8 o'clock, and said 'Don't play the crowd, play your own game, and you'll beat them doing that.'

It's a philosophy I've adopted ever since. I remember a great line from *Chariots of Fire* about young men running the opposition off their feet. I suppose in my case, it's a matter of playing the team they support off their feet and making them applaud me for my football, not pick on me because of who I happen to be in love with.

I understand and accept there are those who are paid to write

I never refuse to sign an autograph, because I know how I felt as a kid when I was turned down.

about me, it's their job. I've been told that there are those who think I've become a little bit too nasty, too aggressive on the pitch, that I've lost sight of what I should be doing and am getting involved in things I shouldn't. I don't agree. I'm doing what I think is right to win matches, and until the gaffer tells me any different, I'll stay the same player. It's his view that I value.

What gets me is when people come on the radio complaining about what I might or might not have done during a game, when they are probably the same people who've been trying to have a go at me. They come on and make comments about what's been said and think it's a great joke. I'm still young, people tend to forget that. Yes, I'm a professional footballer, and I'm well paid, so I suppose I'm fair game, but all I want is fairness in return. I couldn't believe it when the stuff spread to Wembley for the Cameroon game in November. People were chanting 'We only hate Man U'. What's playing for Manchester United got to do with playing for your country?

I actually looked down at one stage and made sure I had the England kit on and not a red shirt with the United crest on it. It amazes me that people can come to Wembley and pay good money to watch an England team that's just qualified for the World Cup and spend all night chanting about Manchester United. Gary Neville and I remarked about it as the game was going along. We thought we were hearing things. It does make you wonder about what makes people tick.

It's a common trend that if people don't know what's going on in your life, they just make things up, thinking they know all about you, when they don't really know anything. I've got an awful lot to live up to as a footballer, without all the extra other stuff that comes at me. People just don't stop and think.

What makes me laugh is that most people would give their right arm to be where I am in football, as well as in other things. Yes, young footballers are among the most fortunate people in the country, but that doesn't mean they haven't worked really hard to get where they are. It hasn't been handed to us. Sportsmen are visible, we're in the public eye all the time and, because of that, we're an easier target than most. A lot of opportunities are thrust at young sportsmen these days and sometimes you don't have time to consider all the implications. I'm fortunate to have people that I trust, like my Dad, Alex Ferguson and my

What has playing for
Manchester United got
to do with playing for
your country?

**The Brylcreem Boy
and, yes, I really
like the stuff.**

**It is important to be
happy with your
endorsements and this
one suits me just fine.**

adviser Tony Stephens, who are taking care of my interests. They know what's best for me, they take care of me and that's very important. Youth and impressionability go together, I understand that, but I'm getting to know what's right and what isn't.

I have been fortunate to get involved with some fantastic contracts, but I take none of them for granted, they are all important to me and my career. The Brylcreem Boy is a wonderful concept, and I am delighted to be working for the company. The same is true of Adidas, with whom I have a very special relationship.

I was at a launch in February of my new boot contract, which runs into the next century. What it is worth is not something I like to talk about, but I hope I offer them the right kind of profile for their boots. That's the way these contracts work, I get on well with them and vice versa. In that connection, image is important. Yes, what people think of me matters, but it is how I behave myself that is vital. I know what I want to be, whom I want to represent and how I would like to be treated. It is all about maturing as a person.

I don't like bad manners, I never have done, which is why I never refuse autographs. I'm not at the top of my profession at the moment, but I am playing for Manchester United and for England, so I suppose I'm getting nearer to the top. People think I've been in the first team for years, but I'm only young and I want to be around for another 10 years or more, so there's a long, long way to go yet.

Eric Cantona

One day he was there, the next I got a call from Gary Neville to say that Eric had left. The only regret I have of the time spent learning so much from Eric was not getting the chance to thank him personally. I think we all felt the same way about him. Eric had such a profound impact on so many of us, and it's when you find yourself in situations on the pitch, doing the things you used to practise for hours with him, that you realise he's still at the club in spirit, if not in person. I was one of those fortunate enough to stay behind with Eric in the afternoons at the Cliff, and learn so much from him. For most of the time it involved crossing the ball for him and I believe the fact that I am considered such a good crosser now is because I was so desperate to get it right for him. If I didn't get it right, I used to be annoyed with myself more than he was annoyed with me. I wanted to have the perfect technique. What Eric stood for was perfection. If Eric had

Joie de

a go at you, it wasn't because he deliberately wanted to be nasty, it was to show you that you shouldn't be content with second best. You should always be striving to do better, to be a better player. To be fair, I wanted to stay back anyway, I'm not one of those who leaves just because formal training has finished.

UMBRO

vivre

Eric Cantona was a great influence on me. Here are three pictures that Liverpool supporters won't like, including the celebrations after the 1996 FA Cup final. I took the corner, Eric scored the winning goal.

Walking out
David Busst's

I don't think Eric has been in contact with the club since he left, apart from
setting up a team to play in a match for the dependants of the Munich air
disaster victims, and that's a shame considering all that he achieved. He
played in the testimonial for David Busst of Coventry the week after the
end of the season, and the next day it was announced that he'd gone.

...the

for testimonial game...

When Gary rang me at home and said, 'Guess what, Eric's retired', I couldn't believe it, even though you were never certain what he was thinking, or what he was going to do next. I don't really know what I would have said to him. Probably something simple like 'Thanks for everything'. Eric was a special person. We didn't really know him as he didn't mix with us. He was there in the morning, he trained, and then he would leave after his extra sessions. Nobody bothered him. He loved a speech though (I'm sure that famous one about the seagulls and the trawlers will never be forgotten). He'd get up at players' private functions and then, in that wonderful accent of his, he'd break into a speech which would mesmerise us. The lads had a little bit of a smile between each other at the way he came across, with all those flamboyant gestures, so unlike the English.

It is impossible to understand or to try to put into words exactly what he did for the club. He made us all better players, he made us want to strive to be better, he brought out the best in us. He was a great team-mate, and a wonderful leader when he was the captain. He loved all of us in his way. It is still strange when he isn't there at the training ground in the morning. It is a void, an empty space and that's weird sometimes, but Eric would realise that Manchester United is bigger than any one person and that the club functions without him.

Teddy Sheringham has come in, a completely different personality, but one who has had just as much of an impact, if in a slightly less demonstrative manner. I suppose I have to mention what happened at Crystal Palace that night when Eric went into the crowd. I was on the bench that night, but I can see it as clearly now and I did that evening.

next day Eric Cantona had left the club!

Looking back on it, I can understand to some extent why he did what he did, when the crowd's abuse of him got so bad that he had to react.

Eric Cantona is one of my all-time heroes, but those whom I remember admiring most from my teenage days are Bryan Robson and Glenn Hoddle. As I've said before, it was when watching United in early 1983, when I was in the Fyfield under-8s with stars in my eyes, that I first saw Robson play. It had a galvanising effect on me. There was something about him I loved to see, the running, the confidence, the strength, the goal scoring and the way the crowd responded to him, was magic for me.

Everything Robbo did looked so powerful, everything Glenn Hoddle did looked so classy. Robbo was hustle and bustle, get in there, make things happen; Glenn sprayed the ball around with both feet, so totally in command of what he was doing, it all seemed to come naturally to him. When I started in the United first team I was the no.24, then I graduated to no.10. To be honest, when Teddy Sheringham arrived and said he wanted no.10, I wasn't too happy at first, but Eric had gone, so no.7 was available, the same number Robbo had worn. So, in my professional career, I've worn the shirts with the same numbers as my two heroes. Can't be bad, can it?

'Everything Glenn Hoddle did looked so classy'

'Everything Robbo did looked so powerful'

Poise and balance – two features of Glenn Hoddle the
player, and two reasons why I admired him so much.

A night
to remember...

Glenn Hoddle hugs me
in Rome after England
qualified for the World
Cup finals.

CHAPTER 6

The Busby Babes

David Pegg

Geoff Bent

Eddie Colman

Tommy Taylor

Liam Whelan

Roger Byrne

Mark Jones

Everywhere around Old Trafford there are reminders of the Busby Babes – there is a commemorative statue of Sir Matt Busby as you first arrive at Old Trafford, and there is the famous clock, which was stopped at four minutes past three on 6 February, 1958, the exact moment the plane bringing the brilliant Manchester United side home from a European Cup semi-final tie against Red Star Belgrade, crashed on a snowbound runway at Munich Airport.

The late, great Sir Matt - a footballing legend. What he did for Manchester United was truly inspirational (above).

The names of the players who died at Munich are there: Duncan Edwards, Geoff Bent, David Pegg, Tommy Taylor, Eddie Colman, Mark Jones, Liam Whelan and the captain, Roger Byrne. It is hard to imagine what the effect of that terrible tragedy must have had on the lives of people in Manchester and across the world. We cannot escape comparisons with the Babes, nor would we want to. They set a standard, which every future generation has to try to live up to. It isn't easy.

It is only when you become part of the United family, that you can truly understand what these players meant to the club. It is hard to imagine, when you think what he achieved in his short career and what was said about his talents at the time, that I'm a year older now than Duncan Edwards was when he died from his injuries. I look at pictures of him and think what a player he must have been. He would definitely have

The late, great Sir Matt – a footballing legend. What he did for Manchester United was truly inspirational (above).

The Babes – lining up before their last match together, the European Cup semi-final, second leg against Red Star at Belgrade in February 1958 (left).

Duncan Edwards

Duncan Edwards – perhaps the greatest of the Babes, what a magnificent player he must have been (right).

played in the 1958 World Cup, but also the 1962, the 1966, the 1970 and possibly more. How much more might United and England have won had they lived?

What a giant of a player he must have been, and all this at the age of 21. The lads - Giggsy, the Nevilles, Nicky Butt, Scholesy and I - often find ourselves discussing the Babes and what it must have been like to be in that group, with the nation marvelling at your talents. I suppose it is possible to think that the nineties group is also making an impact, though we would never be arrogant enough to speak as if we'd taken their place. This is a different era, a different team, but I would like to think the bond between the current crop of young players at United is every bit as special as the one that the fifties team possessed.

☐ CLASS OF '92 . . . the Cup winning United Youth side now on the verge of senior soccer. Back row (l to r): Raphael Burke, Gary Neville, Simon Davies, John O'Kane, Andy Noone, Nicky Butt, Ben Thornley. Front: Robert Savage, David Beckham, George Switzer, Keith Gillespie, Paul Scholes, Chris Casper

I watched a documentary earlier this year that paid tribute to the Babes on the fortieth anniversary of the tragedy and it made me begin to understand how much their passing meant to the public. When I looked at the freshness in the players' faces, of the excitement that it brought them to play for Manchester United, the first English team to play in Europe, it brought the hairs up on the back of my neck.

It showed just how much the history of the club meant to the people and also what a remarkable experience it must have been to have played in that quarter-final second leg against Athletico Bilbao in front of over 50,000 fans in 1957. How young the heart of that team was, how much enjoyment they got from their football! It does seem uncanny that the same feeling of adventure is in our team now.

One of the United fans who followed that team said that watching it play football gave him as much pleasure as the birth of each of his four children. What can you say to that? We have been made aware over recent years of what it takes to win the European Cup and we have a passion in us which drives us to become better and stronger all the time. The Babes were deprived of having the chance to complete their mission of winning the European Cup when they were on the threshold of such a magnificent achievement. Alex Ferguson won't let us rest on our laurels, he's always setting us new targets, telling us we cannot be satisfied with the things we've done in the past, that there's no room for complacency in anything we do, otherwise we won't achieve what we want so much.

I went to the memorial service in Manchester Cathedral the night before we played Bolton on 6 February this year. It was one of the most emotional experiences of my life. From that Friday night onwards, I couldn't get it out of my mind. It was heartbreaking that night to see Duncan Edwards's mum, who is 89. When she went up to the front to light a candle, it really got to me. Bobby Charlton made a very emotional speech as well. It was hard to believe looking at him that he had survived the accident and had gone on to become such an ambassador for Manchester United and England. Then came the match itself, and that was another really incredible occasion.

The players had talked in the dressing room before the game about how we would react when the minute's silence started. I would like to say how much we all appreciated the reaction of the Bolton fans. I know that a few of them have had some pretty nasty reactions to me before, but they were absolutely superb that afternoon, the whole country appreciated it.

We thought we would put our arms across each other's shoulders as we stood inside the centre circle for the minute's silence, but when we walked out behind Bobby and Nat Lofthouse carrying the eight wreaths, we didn't really know whether we would do that or not. In the end, it was a spontaneous response, one of comradeship, to embrace each other. It was nice, symbolic of what we feel about each other as team-mates and friends, and also of what being part of Manchester United means to us.

You can never fully understand what it must have been like to be a young player at Manchester United at that time, or what it meant to their families when they didn't come home after the Belgrade trip; but we are in the United first team, winning championships, leading the way in Europe, flying here, flying there. It means we can relate much more.

There have been a lot of questions asked about us at European Cup level. I'm sure that they posed the same questions about the original Babes forty years ago. I know times and perceptions have changed, but I would like to think that the

New generation of Busby Babes

current generation of United kids can become as much a part of the folklore of football – and cherished as much, though I think that's a lot more difficult these days – as Busby's side. We know we have to work hard to earn people's admiration, and their respect. A lot of ordinary people wish they could be just like us and I understand and appreciate that feeling. I would like everyone to know that we are all dedicated professionals, that playing football means everything to us, we do it for love first, and that the rewards come a long way second. I speak for everyone at Manchester United when I say that.

Perhaps it is because we focus on football first that we get our rewards.

There is a unity of spirit and understanding at United, which is only enhanced when we win things and are successful together. You cannot put a price on the enjoyment, the thrill of scoring goals, of being part of a family that gets things done in an attractive way. Yes, I know that the rewards are great, but you don't get anything out of this world unless you're prepared to work for it.

The essence of Manchester United is working for each other, and never forgetting you're only one part of a team. The moment you think you're bigger and better than anyone else is the moment you're finished. I suppose you could say we're doing pretty well at the moment. That is down to so many different factors. The spirit of Busby prevails, even though time has moved on. Same ideas, different people; same principles,

OUTH ON THEIR SIDE . . . **Manager Eric Harrison with United's youth side**   *Picture: PAUL LEWIS*

a different era in which to carry them through. Which brings me on to the lads themselves.

I suppose you could pick out five of us, myself, the two Nevilles, Gary and Phil, Nicky Butt and Paul Scholes, as we all came through the system together. Ryan Giggs at 24 is a bit of a golden oldie as far as we're concerned, but what a player. First and foremost, Ryan inspired all of us. All the players a little younger than him had so much respect for the kind of player he is, and the way he's handled himself.

He has been at the club for years, and from the moment he broke into the team, we could see what an exceptional player he was. There's no doubt in my mind that Ryan is world class, he has everything a forward player could want, so much skill, but he never gets carried away with anything. He's about as normal as it's possible to be in this game.

There is so much excitement about the way he plays, the movement, the way he can drift in and out of defenders with that wonderful balance. There aren't many players who can run with the ball, control it with so much pace, and make defenders look silly. He takes a lot of stick, but he's not afraid to give it back – he's so perfected that sliding tackle, they should give him the copyright on it. He's such a nice lad, too, Ryan. He's had to handle the comparisons with George Best and that must be quite daunting, especially when he was so young when they were being made. I think he has seen it as a great compliment to him, rather than as a burden. But he just wants to be treated like Ryan Giggs, the footballer, nothing else.

Giggsy the Great – Ryan Giggs is the centre of attention after another spectacular goal.

The rest of the lads grew up together, through the youth system under Eric Harrison, who has probably had more influence on each of us since he came to United than anyone, the manager included. We owe an enormous debt of gratitude to him. I remember from the outset, he wanted you to work, practise and learn, but he put the creed over in a way that we could all understand. We learned all of our good habits from him. There were times when he would give you the most fearsome rollickings, but it was all done because he wanted us to be the best that we could be. I think a lot of the credit for the way we have all developed as players and as people has to go to him. With that kind of upbringing, we couldn't really go wrong. That's true of all of us, in spite of the fact that we're all different as players and people.

Gary Neville and I have been friends all the way through, really from the first time we played in the youth team together. I seem to have spent most of my time at United in Gary's company, we share on away trips, we have a very special friendship - that of best friends. He's the best man at my wedding to Victoria, and no one deserves that more than

A peck on the cheek from Gary Neville after I scored the third goal in the 1990 Charity Shield against Newcastle.

CHAPTER 6

The effects of 'That Goal' sink in. Peter Schmeichel enjoyed his view of it.

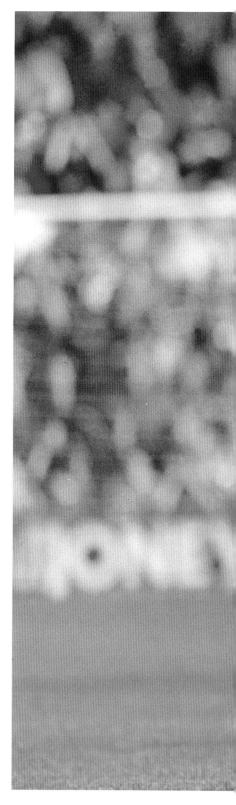

him. It's weird in a way what good friends we've become because our personalities are so different – he's from Bury, and I'm supposed to be the flash Cockney. But we seem to know each other's moods, when we're happy or unhappy, when we need a lift or when we need to be put in our place.

We have a laugh about how we react to goals. When he scored his first for United against Middlesbrough in the 3-3 draw at Old Trafford last season, a vital result for us after being 3-1 down, I was the first to congratulate him. I can remember how I felt about my first goal, but he took it all in his stride. Typical Gary. He's a brilliant guy and a superb player who's always been determined to get what he wants. He won't do anything that might restrict his hopes of progress in football. He's a very sensible person, very level-headed, and he would do anything for you, the kind of guy you'd want on your side every step of the way. His younger brother Phil has come on a bomb. I don't know him as well as I do Gary because he's younger, of course, and came through in a different age group. But Phil is just as dedicated, just as switched on as his brother, they're from really solid stock. Their father, Neville, is the commercial manager

at Bury, and he and his wife have also been there for me if ever I've needed advice. They are a smashing family, the kind of people you'd trust with your life. Nicky Butt is someone else who, if you spoke to him only a couple of times, you'd think was a really quiet guy, but once you get to know him, he's a good laugh, a good personality. I think he's the most improved player at the club this season and, in the absence of Roy Keane, whose injury gutted us all - because he's such a strong guy you don't expect those kind of injuries to happen to him - Nicky has shown what a class player he's become. I think his performance at Chelsea in the third round of the FA Cup this season, when we won 5-3 and were 5-0 up at one stage, underlined his qualities. He was absolutely phenomenal at Stamford Bridge. I was cringing at some of the tackles he was putting in. He gets a knock and he gets up straight away, in a similar vein to David Batty of Newcastle. He just brushes people off and gets on with the game. When I say that Nicky sometimes goes in for 'awful' challenges, I mean the kind of tackles most of us wouldn't dream of making. Frightening, really. But he shouldn't be seen as just a ball-winner, it's a label that's attached itself to Batty as well, and it isn't fair to either of them. Nicky's strength is unbelievable – surely he must have a great chance of being selected for the World Cup squad.

Scholesy is different class, as well. He came to the country's attention in Le Tournoi in the summer of 1997 when he took to international football as if he'd been playing it all his life. He's always been a fantastic player but because he wasn't given as many chances as early as some of the rest of us, maybe people were amazed at how well he did for England. I wasn't. He's something special. When we were in the youth team we used to call him Kenny Dalglish. He was that sort of player, cheeky in the area, a great tackler too. He's quite fierce when he wants to be. He's not far removed from Nicky Butt in the tackling stakes, and there aren't that many who come away with the ball after a challenge with Scholesy. He's a very quiet lad, he doesn't say much. I remember his first England Press conference in France – the Press boys could hardly get a word out of him, so I had to take the brunt of the questions. Not something I really enjoyed but I know what it's like for the first time to look into about 25 faces you don't really recognise. You have to be on the alert all the time because they like to fish for lines from you. Scholesy will be fine, once he gets used to it.

What do the boys think of me? I don't know really. I hope they like me, I think they do. They would soon tell me if I was getting too big for my boots. Definitely. I'd know by the way they were treating me if I was doing anything wrong. I know that they all feel I get a bad deal in the papers a lot of the time, and they feel for me. We stick together – the kind of spirit that is fostered at Manchester United is special.

That Goal, Those Celebra

I wasn't sure if I was starting the 1996-7 season in the first team, even though I'd previously scored a goal I'll never forget, the winner in the FA Cup semi-final against Chelsea, and took the corner from which Eric won us the FA Cup against Liverpool. You never really know with our manager if you're in or not. It was a beautiful day in London; we travelled down for the Wimbledon game the previous evening and I watched the previews to the season. We had won the double so we were the team everyone wanted to beat, but we had also set a standard we knew we had to maintain. That is the Manchester United way and it is always important to start the season well.

I recall the season before we had lost 3-1 to Aston Villa with a particularly young side and the manager was being told he couldn't win anything with kids. Er ... well, we nailed that one. The club had a pretty good record at Selhurst Park and I had scored there every time I had been there in the past, all the goals coming at the end behind which they had built a supermarket.

I was in the side, and we had played some smashing stuff and led 2-0 with a few minutes left.

tions

Jordi Cruyff tried an extravagant shot from just inside the Wimbledon half, but it didn't work for him. Then, in the final couple of minutes, the ball fell to me near the halfway line. To be honest, I can't remember if I took one touch or not, but I had a sense that Neil Sullivan, the Wimbledon goalkeeper, was a little way off his line. I wasn't sure, but I swept the ball up into the air. It seemed to hang there for ages. My Dad, who was behind

the goal, said he was watching it go up when the bloke in front stood up and he didn't see it land in the back of the net. I thought it would be close, because I'd hit it perfectly. On the bench, Alex Ferguson said he was muttering 'Oh, trust him'. A couple of seconds later, I was celebrating one of the most incredible moments of my career.

John Motson, the BBC commentator, described it on *Match of the Day* as 'absolutely phenomenal'. I'd like to thank him for summing it up so succinctly. I don't see myself as a different class of player, but I would like to be thought of as someone with a bit of talent. I hope that in years to come they will think of me and say, 'He could play a bit'. I would like young kids to admire me for what I do. It's not being flash, it's just wanting to make something of a name for myself. I suppose goals like the one at Wimbledon, and a few more besides in the past few seasons, can only help that.

But there I am, in the papers again, over the way I celebrated a couple of goals this season, at Everton and then at Chelsea in the FA Cup. But there is nothing premeditated about it, I don't go out with the intention of celebrating like I do, or causing offence, or getting at anyone in

particular. They just happen. It's instinct, ask any goalscorer and they'll tell you the same. I'm just celebrating a goal, simple as that. If I did do something that affected the other players, or the team as a whole, they'd tell me about it, or they'd be funny with me. I'd know. I don't think the manager would be shy of letting me know either. I wouldn't do anything like that. The incident that drew most of the criticism came at Chelsea in the FA Cup tie. I think it's only fair that I should be allowed to tell my side of the story and put the record straight.

One paper said a few days after the game that I was a Boy Wonder who was getting too big for my boots. The rest of the lads couldn't believe what they were reading. I was shown the article. It was absolutely unbelievable. The boss is always the first to say that he loves to see us celebrate goals, because they're so special to us and to him and the club. He sometimes has a go at you if you don't celebrate them, especially as a team. It's the kind of delight in each other's successes he likes to see.

The celebration that caused

most antagonism – and certainly the most pictures – was of the one with my hands behind my ears after the first goal of our five at Stamford Bridge this season. There was no malice intended, I wasn't trying to get at anyone, I just think I'd been getting a bit of stick and I wanted to show that it hadn't affected me. More than that it was my sheer delight at scoring and putting us ahead. Whatever happens in the future I shan't do it again. The point has been made.

But I can't help the way I react, it shows how much I care for the team and that we are playing well. Football is one of the most important things in my life. It has got me where I am today, so of course I care about it. I love to win too, and that's why I love to let it show. Goalscoring has always been a buzz for me, whether it's been for my local Sunday side, or United. I try to keep a sense of fun about things, but it's a business as

well and it's important for me to score and feel I'm contributing to the team.

That afternoon at Chelsea was something a bit special. I don't think I've ever known us to be more 'up' for a match. We went out there thinking 'this is it'. We had let ourselves down at Coventry the previous weekend, and I was talking to Teddy Sheringham about it the night before the Cup tie and we hardly needed to say anything to each other to understand exactly how we were both feeling. This was going to be our game. We wanted to win it, desperately. The word used for our performance that afternoon was 'awesome' and that is right, it was awesome. It was wonderful to be involved in a brilliant performance like that – 5-0 up against an in-form team. I think it told people everything they needed to know about how good this United team is and how we believe it can become even better.

We have certain standards, of course, but we discovered that day that we can improve further. It's about keeping a level head and, not getting carried away. I remember coming off at half-time for two contrasting reasons – a brief, niggly conversation with Frank Leboeuf was followed a few seconds later by Gianluca Vialli, a footballer for whom I have a tremendous respect, coming up, shaking my hand and saying, 'You are a very good player.' Unbelievable really, when you consider what he has achieved in his career. I was shocked and delighted. One of the best things in this world is to find out how much those for whom you truly have respect appreciate your talents. Coming from Vialli, I couldn't have been paid a better compliment, nor one I appreciated more.

(Chelsea 3 – Man Utd 5)

CHAPTER 7

And now he is the player-manager of Chelsea, after the stunning departure of Ruud Gullit. It is remarkable how these things turn around sometimes, but from a player's point of view, I believe the more stability there is in a club, the better it has to be. I have only played for one manager. Everyone at United has a clear sense of what is required, what is needed. We know how to behave, how to handle ourselves in public, what we should and shouldn't say, and we know what it means to be a Manchester United player.

Whatever the reasons for his departure, I think that Ruud Gullit made Chelsea a very exciting side. They won the FA Cup in 1997 playing some terrific football, they beat us at Old Trafford in the League, they have a blend of brilliant foreign players and some outstanding youngsters like Jody Morris and Danny Granville. I hope that they continue to do well now that Gullit has gone because we thrive on the kind of challenge they can offer us.

Of course, we couldn't be expected to maintain that sort of standard every week. I don't believe any team on earth can.

A couple of weeks after beating Chelsea, we were beaten at home by
Leicester, who have always given us a hard time and who are one of the
most improved teams in the country. I am one of those people who take
defeat pretty well; I don't go moping on about it. If we are beaten, or we
draw, or we don't play well on a Saturday, by Monday morning I'm as
bright as a button again.

Football means the world to me but there are more important things
to do in life than come down on yourself too much for losing a football
match. Of course I'll be upset, but I don't carry it on.

Walking away with
the Charity Shield!
Always a great way
to start the season.

CHAPTER 8

Europe

The European experience has been magnificent for all of us, and for me there are special memories. I scored my first senior goal for Manchester United against Galatasaray in the Champions' League at Old Trafford at the Stretford End, on 7 December 1994. I wouldn't say it was one of the classics – I half-hit the ball across the goalkeeper, but I can remember the sensation of scoring. The moment that Eric and I celebrated it, we were captured by a brilliant photograph leaping at each other and embracing in mid-air, which was a lot more difficult an act to perform than scoring the goal itself! The best way I can think of describing my debut goal for United was that I couldn't keep a smile off my face for a couple of days afterwards. At the time the goal went in my Dad was so excited that he jumped up and head-butted the guy in the row behind him. I think Mum just cried her eyes out. She couldn't stop telling the people around her that I was her son.

You can hardly begin to imagine what effect the goal had on me, but I think the rest of the lads were as delighted for me as I was for myself. We won the game 4-0, but it wasn't to be for us that season. We had been thrashed 4-0 in Barcelona the month before and didn't reach the quarter-final stages. Inevitably there were more theories that we didn't have the quality, that English football was still way behind the major nations of Europe. But we knew how close we were getting, and how much respect we were gathering as a team.

It has been said that winning the European Cup is the manager's great dream, but it is the same for all of us. We have come a long way together, but can you imagine, with so many of us in our early twenties, others still in their teens, what it would mean to be fêted as the best team in Europe?

later was a night none of us will be allowed to forget, when United lost their 40-year unbeaten home record. We had been warned by the manager until he was blue in the face never to take any team too lightly. We had won 2-0 in Istanbul against them in the first leg where I scored one of the

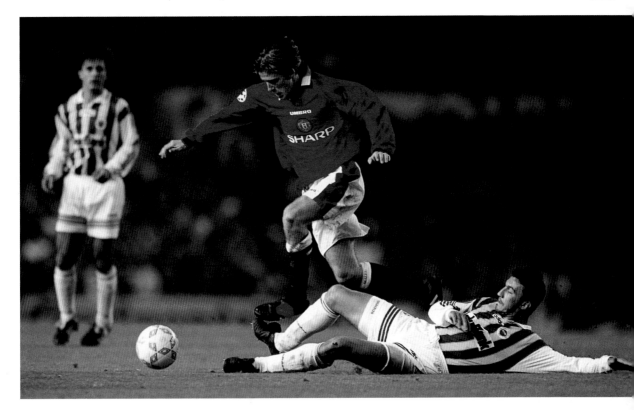

There have been times when we haven't done ourselves justice and we are the first people to acknowledge that. We didn't play particularly well in Turin in September 1996, when we lost 1-0 in the first game of the series against Juventus, and that set us back a bit. Fenerbahce a month

goals – we had been into the lion's den and emerged with a victory. Maybe we took too much for granted, I don't know, but we came unstuck in a big way going down 1-0 to a goal in the 78th minute. No one likes to think they will be remembered as part of the team that lost United's proud

A nightmare for United as we lost the club's unbeaten home record in Europe.

We beat Rapid Vienna to reach the quarter finals of the Champions' League.

unbeaten home record in Europe. It's certainly not something I'm particularly proud of, but we have to hold up our hands and admit that the Turkish side was excellent on the night, and we were way below our usual standard. When the goal went in I could feel the sense of disbelief in the ground. It was as though Old Trafford was frozen for a moment. The result also meant we had to get something from our trip to Vienna in December to make certain we qualified. I suppose the greatest lesson I've learned from my experience of European football is that you can never relax for a second. I know it's repeating an old cliché, but if you give the ball away in the Premiership, even to the best teams, because the pace of the game is so fast, you're going to get it back pretty quickly. In Europe, make a mistake, and they'll run your legs off.

Against Juventus at home a month later, we played some superb football in the second half, although the damage had been done by their penalty. Nevertheless we reached the semi-final after first beating Vienna away, on a freezing cold night – I supplied a cross for the second goal which Eric Cantona scored superbly to put us through –

and then on one of the most thrilling nights I can ever remember at Old Trafford, by beating FC Porto, the champions of Portugal in the quarter-final. They had been unbeaten in their qualifying group, winning 3-2 in AC Milan with two goals from Jardel, a very imposing young striker. They had won all three of their away games, so the fact that we had been drawn at home first didn't seem to give us any special favours.

It turned out to be one of those very special occasions, the kind which come along maybe twenty times in your life if you're lucky. The whole team clicked. OK, we might have been helped a little because they had a goalkeeper named Hilario who didn't exactly have a great night, but that would be taking too much away from the lads.

I thought Giggsy was magnificent that night and his goal, the third, was a beautiful effort... the build-up, the finish, the confidence, the cheek that Ryan had. We won 4-0, and by easing up a little in the second leg after we had weathered a couple of early dangerous moments, we held out pretty comfortably for a goalless draw. The semi-final beckoned.

Celebrating one of the great European goals at Old Trafford.

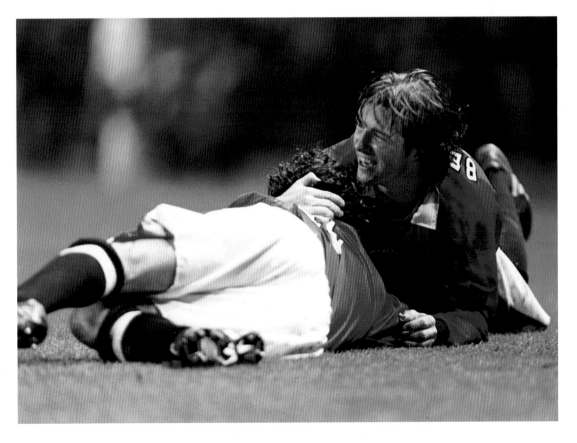

CHAPTER 8

I can hardly believe the fact that we lost to a team we were clearly better than.

Our opponents were the German Borussia Dortmund. We knew they would be tough – has there ever been a German team that rolled over and let you play? We knew that big Peter Schmeichel was having problems with his back and was going out on the field before the game for a fitness test. He didn't make it. We had every confidence in his deputy, the Dutchman Raymond Van Der Gouw, who had waited a long time for a chance like this. We knew he wouldn't let us down.

I remember we had so much of the game but couldn't score. A great move ended with Nicky Butt hitting the post and the ball was scrambled away. I was beginning to think that 0-0 wouldn't be a bad score at all when one of their subs had a pop from about 30 yards, the ball took a wicked deflection off Pally, I think it was, and flew into the top corner. There was nothing Raymond could do about it. A 1-0 defeat in a game we should have at least drawn, probably won. We were all bitterly disappointed.

The second leg was an even greater letdown. I don't think anyone in the country – even those who couldn't give a monkeys whether Manchester United won the European Cup or not – really thought we wouldn't make it to the final. I read that the manager was asked if he felt the whole of the country was behind us, and he laughed. The old, you either love Manchester United or you hate them, routine again.

But we were really confident, because there hadn't been anything in Borussia's performance in the first leg which had worried us unduly. We knew they were technically good, but they hadn't offered much of a threat on their own ground and at Old Trafford, with 50,000 behind us, they would be under the cosh from the word go. I can't remember a more frustrating night, even the defeat to Fenerbahce wasn't as much of a blow to the pit of the stomach as this 1-0 defeat. We really thought we were going to win the European Cup, there was a special feeling about the club, we had never felt better in ourselves, nor more

Nicky Butt and I try to come to terms with the significance of our defeat.

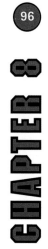

Showing a clean pair of heels in Kosice.

confident. The fact that Borussia went on to beat Juventus in the final left me feeling even more gutted, but they truly deserved it because they were magnificent on the night.

It has to be said that any team which defeats Manchester United home and away and then Juventus in a one-off game deserves everything it gets and there can be no fairer way of paying tribute to Borussia. I just hope they're keeping the European Cup warm for us.

It's taken time for United to believe that no team in Europe is unbeatable – there have been enough harsh lessons on the way – but I certainly believe there's a new-found level of belief in the players at the club. Our performance at Old Trafford against Juventus this season couldn't have shown that belief up much more dramatically. We were so much up for the match, that to go a goal down after 20 seconds shook us all, and could have shattered our confidence if we hadn't had such great self-belief. We proved that night, not just to fans of United and those in England, but to those all over the world, that teams aren't

United are back! We finally laid the ghost of our defeat to Juventus the previous year to rest.

unbeatable, and that we have a right to be rated up there as one of the very best in Europe.

On the away trip to Juventus too, I could tell by the atmosphere in the dressing room before the game that we never doubted ourselves for a minute. OK, we didn't win that night, but we reached the last eight,

and had taken another significant step forward. A lot of players felt vindicated that night, as though they had exorcised the ghost of the performances in Barcelona and Turin, that they had taken all the flak that was flying around then and had made a point. From a personal point of view, I've found all the European experiences fascinating – the varied challenges, the different conditions and atmospheres, the opportunity to pit your talents against the best players in Europe. I have learned from them all – how could you not when you're playing against such class players as Alessandro Del Piero and Zinedine Zidane of Juventus? You can only profit from playing out there in close proximity to people of their talent, watching players like that closely – even though you're playing against them – picking up their best habits, and then practising them yourself. A bit like going back to Eric Cantona and his dedication to practice. I have a very special admiration for Del Piero.

Experiences on foreign fields have helped build me as a player.

He not only looks the part, but he has such superb close control, he turns defenders so well, and his range of passing is superb. I was fortunate enough to be able to take part in a special advertisement with him in Seville last December for Pepsi. We had the opportunity to spend quite a bit of time together. What a great guy, brilliant. His English wasn't as good as Vialli's, but he couldn't have been more friendly, asking me how I was and what I'd been doing, though he seemed to know from watching TV what I'd been up to anyway! You can imagine what it's like for a lad of 22 to find out how much interest someone like Del Piero is taking in their progress. Some people have been kind enough to say that I've made the sort of impression on English football that he's made on the Italian game. It's a quite unbelievable compliment. Paolo Maldini of AC Milan, the Italian captain, was also at the Pepsi photo-shoot, and he's another of the players I greatly admire.

Tussling with Alessandro Del Piero, one of the greatest young players in Italy.

CHAPTER 9

Playing for England

I had a sneaking feeling I might have made it into the squad for the 1996 European Championships. I thought my form had been good for United, but Terry Venables didn't seem to have noticed me that much. I remember too, that when I was a young kid having trials with Tottenham, and he was the manager, he'd only ever come to see me once, whereas Alex Ferguson was always there, taking an interest, making me feel so much a part of the United family.

Euro 96 was a brilliant tournament, although I was disappointed not to have played any part of it. I watched in awe as England almost qualified for the final. I couldn't even begin to appreciate the kind of heartache that someone like Gareth Southgate must have been feeling after that penalty against Germany in the semi-finals. To be honest, I wanted to be as far away as I could from the matches, that's just the way I was feeling. I hoped it wouldn't be long before it was my chance. When Glenn Hoddle replaced Terry Venables as England coach, my attitude brightened considerably. I don't know why, I just had a feeling I had a better chance with Glenn than with Terry Venables.

What can I really say about the day I was chosen for the squad for the first time? The call came from Glenn Hoddle to Alex Ferguson who summoned me into his office to tell me I had been chosen. My heart began to race, I was so proud and I could hardly wait to rush out and call my parents. I knew how happy they would be for me. In the England squad at 21, not bad, until a certain Michael Owen came along!

So when Glenn Hoddle chose his first squad as the England coach, my name was in it. I think my Dad bought ten copies of all the national newspapers the next morning, and kept Teletext on the screen all night long, staring at my name.

Moldova v. England
1 SEPTEMBER 1996

The first match under Glenn was a World Cup qualifier against Moldova. I didn't have the foggiest where the place was so I had to look it up – a small republic tucked in between Romania and Russia. Although we weren't sure what to expect and thought that they might prove a tough hurdle, on paper it wasn't a match expected to cause England too many problems.

We gathered at the Burnham Beeches hotel, England's HQ for quite a few years and although I've never been a nervous person (certainly not before matches) that was a little bit of an ordeal. There was Stuart Pearce, Paul Merson, Tony Adams and Paul Gascoigne, people I had watched and supported as England players, and now I was in their company. It took

a little bit of getting used to.

I soon got accustomed to the banter, it's no different from club level, and at least I had Gary Neville to help me through and introduce me to everyone. It didn't take long for me to feel part of the group. Gazza is great company, a real livewire, always talking, always upbeat, always wanting to know about you and how you've been playing. He keeps the lads on their guard every minute. I'd heard all about his practical jokes.

Even when I'm relaxing, as above with Paul Ince, there's still time to practise some fancy footwork.

Learning at the feet of the master. Glenn Hoddle shows he has all the skills that entranced me as a youngster.

Then came something rather special. At the end of our first training session together, with no cameras around, and the rest of the players already back on the coach, the manager called me across and we sat in the centre circle of the training pitch at Bisham Abbey, just Glenn and I, talking. He was getting me as high as he could, getting my confidence up, telling me what the England situation was going to be about. I hadn't been thinking too much about the game at that point, then he told me I was playing. This was the Wednesday, before we left for Moldova the next day. He told me why he was playing me and where, to get me settled into the idea.

My first training session with England followed by a personal chat with the manager, and he tells me I'm in the team, making my debut! I can't ever remember getting such special treatment before. Gary was a bit envious, because I seemed to be the one who was always being taken to one side for a chat about how I was playing, how I felt, that kind of thing. I've read about how Glenn felt that when he was an England player, he wasn't used as well as he thought he should be. His is the kind of single-minded determination that Alex Ferguson has always shown at United. The two of them are very different, but so much alike. They know exactly what they want, and they get the players on their side, straight away. I went back to the hotel feeling absolutely terrific. I think I could have taken on the world, let alone Moldova. My only regret was that my Mum and Dad weren't there to see the game, but there wasn't any way they could get to a place like Moldova.

Of the new players in the squad, there were to be two debuts in Chisinau – Andy Hinchcliffe of Everton and myself. The country itself wasn't the most wonderful I've ever visited. I read in one of the papers when we got home about a children's orphanage near Chisinau, and how terrible the conditions were there. The senior squad had a collection before we played Moldova at home, and I hope we did something to make children's lives there a little easier. It reminded me again how insignificant it is to be pictured walking a dog. There was a kind of dark brown water running in the hotel – Gary and I couldn't believe it. I think it was the first foreign trip where I've actually read a book, cover to cover. I'm not a great book reader, I can't even remember the name of it, but it kept my mind off the country and the food. Not somewhere I'd choose for a holiday. There was nothing to do or see. We only ever went out together in the coach, there's no such thing as strolling the streets, which is a bit of a shame, but that's life. It was hotel, training pitch, back to hotel, meal and bed.

England 3 (Barmby, Gascoigne, Shearer) Moldova 0

Moldova: Romanencu, Secu, Nani, Testimitanu, Gaidamasluc, Epureanu, Curteanu, Belous (Sischin), Clescenco, Mitereu (Rebeja), Popovici.

England: Seaman, G Neville, Pearce, Ince, Pallister, Southgate, Beckham, Gascoigne (Batty), Shearer, Barmby (Le Tissier), Hinchcliffe. (Ferdinand).

ATTENDANCE: 9,000.

The proudest kid in the country, as I made my England debut in Chisinau.

The game itself wasn't a classic but the Moldovans weren't afraid of us, they had bags of enthusiasm, they worked for each other, and their technique was good, as the Italians would find out later. I didn't have that great a game, but Gary did really well, crossing for the first goal, scored by Nicky Barmby. Gazza got the second, Alan Shearer the third and we'd done the job we'd been asked to do. I remember not being nervous at all, everyone had been buoying me up, but I just knew I had to play like I'd been doing for United. The boss played me out on the right, so there was nothing special to have to get used to. Considering it was a World Cup qualifier, and we hadn't had any time to get to know each other that well, it was a tremendous result for us.

CHAPTER 9

England v. Poland

9 OCTOBER 1996

I was made aware by quite a few of the lads that Poland was going to be a tough nut to crack. They had been for a long time to a number of

England sides. This team was to be no different. The manager told us before the match that they were no slouches, we'd have to be aware of them, but that it was up to us to set the tempo of the game. That is what Wembley demands of England teams, it seems. This wasn't my first experience of the Twin Towers, but the first in an England shirt and it felt different. I've never been one to be consumed by nerves before the kick-off and I wasn't on this occasion, only as proud as punch to be representing my country at home for the first time. I couldn't even begin to think what a proud moment it must have been for the rest of my family.

There were a couple of changes from the side which won in Moldova – Les Ferdinand and Steve McManaman were in. It was a team bursting with attacking options. Unfortunately we started really sluggishly. I don't know why. Before I'd even touched the ball, we were behind. Gary said he didn't react quickly enough, but it was hard for anyone to be to blamed as we were all a bit sloppy, and they suddenly took the lead. My first England game at home, and we're a goal behind after seven minutes. It certainly concentrates the mind. Then we started to knock the ball around with a

bit more urgency. I got a couple of good feels of the ball and when Gazza was brought down, and the free-kick rebounded out to me a few yards into their half, I caught sight of Alan Shearer towards the edge of the area. All those endless hours spent knocking the ball in from various angles and distances paid off, the ball curled towards the edge of the area and Alan was in on it, his header firm and true. We were level.

Just about to pick out Alan Shearer for the opening goal against Poland (left).
The skipper shows his appreciation (above).

Captain Fantastic had done it again, but it was courtesy of a Beckham cross. Another one for my grandad's scrapbook. Then, a few minutes before half-time when the ball broke between Alan and Les on the edge of the area, the captain was in like a shot, and what a shot! David Seaman had to make one stunning save a couple of minutes later, but we went in for the interval 2-1 ahead. There were a couple of alarms in the second half, by everyone's consent it wasn't one of England's better performances, but we were two games, two wins and rolling.

England 2 (Shearer 2) Poland 1 (Citko).

England: Seaman, G Neville, Pearce, Ince, Southgate (Pallister), Hinchcliffe, Beckham, Gascoigne, Shearer, Ferdinand, McManaman.

Poland: Wozniak, Waldoch, Zielinski, Jozwiak, Hajto, Michalski, Baluszynski, Wojtala, Nowal, Citko, Warzycha (Sagamowski).

ATTENDANCE: 74,663

Georgia might not have been much of a place, but we got the result we wanted, a victory which kept our qualifying hopes on track.

Georgia v. England
9 NOVEMBER 1996.

The longest, most uncomfortable plane journey of all time. It seemed to take for ages to get to Tblisi and the thing that stuck in most of our minds as we came in to land, was that we couldn't see any lights in the place. It was like a city plunged into darkness. I'm not a snob, but I would say that I like a bit of luxury when it comes to hotels and food (then again I'm talking while tucking into a Big Mac and fries and I've just stepped into a plate of ketchup on the floor!). The hotel in Tblisi was, I am told, about as good as it gets, but I didn't think much of it. I don't suppose the FA thought much of my phone bill home either, the cost of calls was outrageous. Everyone mentioned it, even the Press boys. The game itself was really important, especially because there was no Alan Shearer in the side, and people were questioning how we'd score goals.

In the build up to the game, I heard from one or two of the lads that Tony Adams had bared his soul and given a revealing interview into how he'd beaten his alcohol problems. It must have

taken enormous guts to tell a room full of relative strangers what was going on in his life. I don't think I could face up to things in quite the courageous way he did, but then again Tony's that much older than me, he's had a lot more experience of life. I was beginning to realise what comes with the territory of being an England player. There are times when you have to discuss things in public that you would prefer to keep private. Tony obviously felt this was the time to say something. I had always looked on him with a tremendous amount of respect, but it grew a hundred-fold after that.

Tony is a fantastic leader of men, a player with a great passion for his football, who comes alive when he puts on his football strip. There is no one more committed to England. I may not show exactly how proud I am to represent my country, but you can see it in everything Tony Adams does. Gary Neville thinks the big man is magic, he's in awe of him and rightly so.

The game itself was a real triumph for us in testing circumstances and certainly my best away game in the qualifying campaign. Glenn Hoddle had made it clear to us that we would face a potentially hostile crowd, and that Georgia didn't have just one player of Georgi Kinkladze's talents to watch for, there were about half a dozen just as able to turn a game. I was played wide on the right again, with responsibilities to get forward as often as I could, but I had to be very disciplined. I have to say, if I was given the choice, my preference is to play inside slightly, but I understand, too, that it can't be that way at the moment. When I first started in my junior days and I was an outside right, my youth team manager said I could cross the ball better than any seven or eight year old he'd ever seen, but I loved it when I could move into central midfield, as I did in my early teens. I realise I'm never going to be an outside right for Manchester United in the mould of Steve Coppell or Andrei Kanchelskis. It's not really my game to knock the ball past the full back and take him on for pace, though I'll do it if I think there's a chance of beating him, or if I sense he might be nervous. The central role fascinates me, because I think it's in there where you can have most control over a game. When

Roy Keane was injured earlier this season, though it was a really heavy blow for the team, I thought it might be my chance, but I understood when the manager decided that it was Nicky Butt and Paul Scholes' chance for their breakthrough. And what a great attitude and character they've shown. Still, it feels a little isolated at times, out on the right, but if it's what the team needs, it's OK by me. Alex Ferguson and now Glenn

Georgia 0
England 2 (Sheringham, Ferdinand)

Georgia: Zoidze, Lobjanidze, Tskhadadze, Shelia, Gogichaishvili, Nemsadze, Jamarauli, Kinkladze, Kobishavili (Ghudushauri), Arveladze (Gogrichiani), Ketsbaia.

England: Seaman, Campbell, Hinchcliffe, Ince, Adams, Southgate, Beckham, Gascoigne, Ferdinand (Wright), Sheringham, Batty.

ATTENDANCE: 48,000.

Hoddle have both used me in that flank position, and I'm not about to argue with either of them. I just want to play for Manchester United and England and wherever they decide is my best role is fine by me. On this occasion wide on the right, I would like to think the manager was delighted with the way I played – I made more tackles and more interceptions in that game than I think I've ever done. The crowd was wild at the start, but we scored twice in the first half through Teddy Sheringham, who played superbly, and then Les Ferdinand breaking through on the left-hand side, using all his physical strength and scoring with a cracking shot typical of Ferdy. I don't think we heard a peep from the crowd after that, we had killed the game and all their enthusiasm for their own side disappeared. I think they even began cheering some of our better moves and we seemed to have won them over. I don't think David Seaman had to make more than a couple of saves. The flight home took more than six hours but I don't think anyone noticed.

Three wins out of three was as good as it could possibly be. Now it was back to Manchester United, with a couple of months to concentrate on the Premier League, make certain we qualified for the quarter-finals of the Champions' League and then re-focus on England again next February – and the Italians.

The period in between these matches went so fast. In the League, during December and January we had three draws and six victories, one of which, against Tottenham on 12 January, included another one of those goals you remember for a long time. Actually, I was feeling so bad before that game I could hardly walk. I can't remember which leg the pain was in, but I felt really bad. I didn't tell anyone about it, actually, but I took a couple of Paracetamol before the game and as I got into it, the pain subsided. I don't think I was even 50 per cent fit. Not even the boss knows to this day how bad I was feeling, because I didn't want to tell him. I knew I could get through the game, something was inspiring me to play – maybe because it was Tottenham, my grandad's team, at White Hart Lane, and I knew he'd be watching and I wanted to do something special. The goal was one of those spectacular ones, from about 35 yards, straight into the top corner. Ian Walker didn't have a chance. I picked the ball up just inside the centre circle, and took a couple of strides forward. As I struck it, I instinctively knew it was going to be one of those goals. Sorry Grandad. The camera focused on the manager, who was caught mouthing something about it being a fantastic goal. At least, I think that's what he was saying!

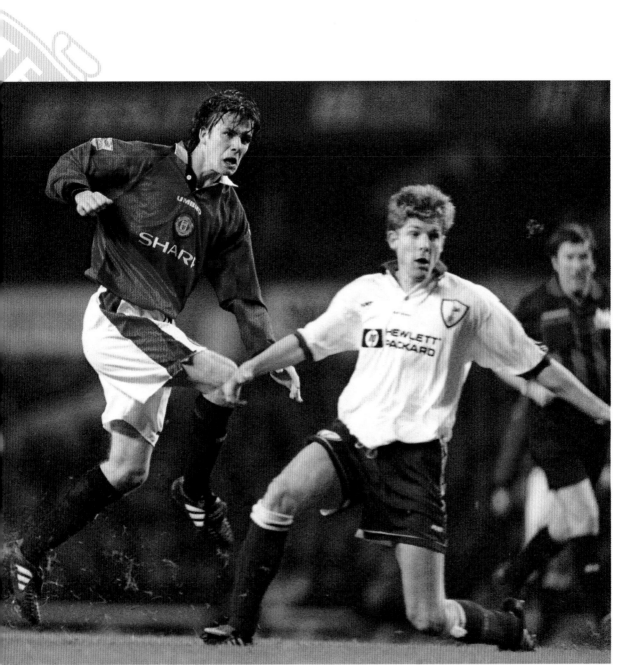

Between the England games, there was the
little matter of keeping our title ambitions on
track. The game at Tottenham gave me another
of 'those' goals and good reason to celebrate.
Sorry Grandad.

Nothing really went right for us against Italy. I felt as though I was detached out on the wing. I never really got going at all.

England v. Italy
12 FEBRUARY 1997

Remember, we had won our first three games, but the victory over Poland at home was said to have been unconvincing. We knew that as well, and Glenn had told us in no uncertain terms that we couldn't be as sloppy again. The build-up to the Italy game was incredible. It seemed as though the media interest had trebled, there were cameras at every session, and the Italian press had turned out in force. I was getting a lot of attention, but the Football Association made certain that when I was asked to go and meet the Press, they could only ask me questions about football, none of the private stuff. They look after you extremely well, we're chaperoned at the conferences, and the young ones, especially, are always grateful for that.

Most of the Italians wanted to know whether I would be playing in Italy at some stage in my future, and whether I thought the arrival in the Premiership of players like Gianfranco Zola, Gianluca Vialli and Roberto di Matteo had had any benefits for English players. Clearly, they have benefited Chelsea enormously,

and I think – like the effect Eric Cantona had on the young players at Manchester United – that their brilliant attitude and appreciation of what it takes to stay at the top of their profession has its effect on younger players. I have a special admiration for Zola who is so dangerous around the penalty area with his wonderful variation at free-kicks. I have studied his dead-ball kicking very closely, I think he must practise them almost as much as me! So, yes, we knew the Italians would be very difficult. They have proved over the years in the biggest matches that they have a knack of producing that little extra something when needed.

It was going to be my first experience of playing against Paolo Maldini, rightly regarded among his peers as the best left-back in world football. We had to make changes. David Seaman was injured, as was Andy Hinchcliffe and there was no Gazza. Steve McManaman and Matt Le Tissier were called into the side. Despite the extra attention, there was nothing different in our preparation. We were told what the team would be at the usual time, and Glenn made the point that we should keep it as quiet as we could – he had special reasons for not wanting the Italians to discover what it was.

I told my Mum and Dad,

> ### England 0 Italy 1 (Zola).
>
> **England:** Walker, G Neville, Pearce, Ince, Campbell, Batty (Wright), McManaman (Merson), Le Tissier (Ferdinand), Shearer, Beckham, Le Saux.
>
> **Italy:** Peruzzi, Ferrara, Costacurta, Cannavaro, De Livio, Dino Baggio, Albertini, Di Matteo, Maldini, Zola (Fuser), Casiraghi (Ravanelli).
>
> ATTENDANCE: 75,055.

and they were sworn to secrecy. A couple of papers had a stab at the identity, some got Matt Le Tissier in, others didn't have him. We knew he was in and we were all comfortable with it. There was no doubt in our minds that we'd win the game and I wasn't nervous about it at all. But things weren't to work out as we had planned. The Italians were superb, their movement was something to behold and they were really up for the game. We never really got into a groove and they seemed to be a shade quicker to the ball than we were. Nothing more than that. Then the goal came, a brilliant ball forward from Costacurta – another superb defender – and a great finish by Zola. He was onto it like a flash, getting onto our wrong side, and punishing us. Sol Campbell tried to tackle him and I think he got a touch, because I felt Ian Walker had it covered.

Alessandro Costacurta pulls my shirt and appeals for a free-kick at the same time.

After that we tried to shake things up. Les Ferdinand came on for Matt Le Tissier and Paul Merson for Steve McManaman, but we couldn't find a way through. The atmosphere at the end was odd, a lot like the one at Old Trafford when we had been beaten by Fenerbahce. No one could quite believe it. I recall later that night, watching it again and seeing Glenn come on TV saying that the result hadn't shaken his confidence one little bit, that he was certain we would qualify, but we had just made the task harder for ourselves. To see a manager so confident after a result that must have hurt him like hell gave me a shot in the arm as well. It might all rest on the final game in Rome, but there was no way the manager wasn't looking to qualify first from the group. Beaten yes, but not broken.

The Italians had two games before we played again, beating Moldova reasonably easily at home, but struggling in Poland for a goalless draw. I thought the Poles should have won the game, and we knew exactly how difficult the task was going to be for us when we went there in the spring. But first we had Georgia at home.

England v. Georgia
30 APRIL 1997

We knew that this was a match we just couldn't lose. After the setback against Italy, it was imperative we used our next home game, against Georgia, to make a point or two back. In our previous two games at Wembley we had been caught cold, and Glenn stressed the importance of being solid from the start, of not giving anything away, of keeping our shape, while setting a strong tempo. It was definitely my best game for England at Wembley, one when I felt I got to grips with everything I was asked to do. I struck the ball well, I felt my touch was good, and my balance just right.

Teddy Sheringham gave us the lead with a fine header just before half-time. We didn't really let the Georgians have a sniff of the ball in dangerous areas and when, in the last minute we got a free-kick inside the area for obstruction, Teddy backheeled the ball and Alan Shearer fizzed it into the top corner. To my mind,

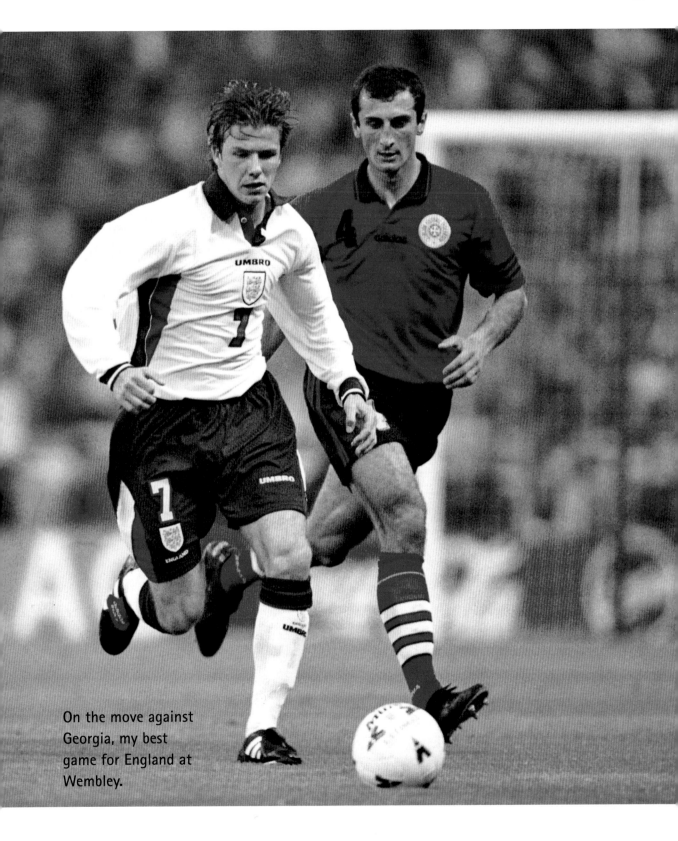

On the move against
Georgia, my best
game for England at
Wembley.

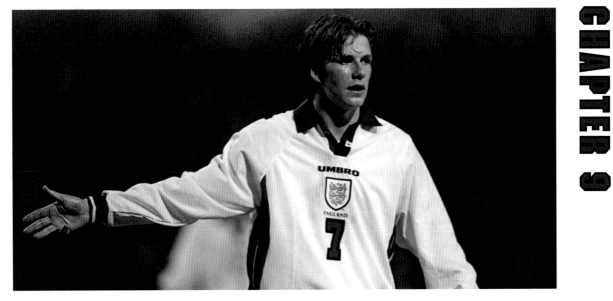

it was an emphatic final statement – that we were back in the group with a vengeance. It was good to see Jamie Redknapp coming back into the international fold for a few minutes near the end. I have a tremendous regard for Jamie as a player. He has been cursed by injuries when he's played for England and I hoped this was going to be a turning point for him. I think he could play in a variety of positions and it was fascinating to hear Glenn talking about the potential use of Jamie as a sweeper in future. It was exciting to think that I could be a part of an England side that had the talents to be so adaptable. Even the fact that Italy defeated Poland 3-0 the same night, and stayed four point clear in the group, couldn't dampen our spirits.

Alan Shearer scored with a spectacular last-minute free-kick, worthy of the celebration (left). Asking for the ball to be played quicker (above).

England 2 (Sheringham, Shearer) Georgia 0

England: Seaman, G Neville, Le Saux, Batty, Campbell, Adams (Southgate), Lee, Ince (Redknapp), Shearer, Sheringham, Beckham.

Georgia: Zoidze, Chikhradze, Shequiladze, Tskhadadze, Shelia, Machavariani (Gogrichiani; A Arveladze), Nemsadze, Jamarauli, Ketsbsaia, Kinkladze (Gakhokidze), S Arveladze.

Another Championship for the mighty Reds. What a great feeling it is to be Champions of the country, which shows as I lift the Premiership trophy.

Manchester United won the Premiership title again less than a month later, our fourth in five seasons and a remarkable achievement for the club. It was an incredible season. We were all absolutely stunned when Kevin Keegan left Newcastle in January. They had pushed us all the way the previous year, they were even 12 points ahead at one stage, but we pegged them back and pegged them back, and they fell away. I remember seeing how Kevin reacted after a Monday night match against Leeds, when he got all upset about certain things our manager had been saying about the title race. The Press loved it, of course, turning it into some sort of psychological warfare between the two men. To me, it just showed what pressures managers are under and what a wonderful job Alex Ferguson has done to keep winning trophies for Manchester United while others just dream about them.

Howard Wilkinson had left Leeds earlier in the season, Joe Royle was to leave Everton in March, Graeme Souness departed from Southampton, and we just kept on winning. Well, almost. We knew it was likely we would have to play four games in nine days at the end of the season, and we made a bit of a fuss about it. Players tend to just get on with it, they don't get involved in the politics. If the manager says play, and we're fit, we play. A couple of days after our depressing 1-0 defeat to Borussia in the European Cup semi-final, we went to Ewood Park and beat Blackburn 3-2. We had been top since February, but we were only three points ahead of Arsenal now, and the race was getting tight.

I think the title really turned in our favour on 19 April, when we had a morning kick-off against Liverpool at Anfield. I'm not one of those who likes morning starts, in fact I hate them. It can throw your whole system, but Liverpool is Liverpool whatever time of the day or night and this was another game we were really up for. I don't know what it is about Anfield, but it brings out the very best in us. We pushed forward confidently from the start, and from two of my corners, one from either side, big Pally scored with brilliant headers, right in front of the Kop. When Andy Cole scored a third, midway through the second half, we were well on the way. I think we won the title that morning.

I suppose it shows how perverse football can be that we should actually win it without playing at all. Liverpool lost at Wimbledon and Newcastle, who were pushing up fast behind us, drew 0-0 at West Ham. Newcastle actually got second place in the League, and qualified for the

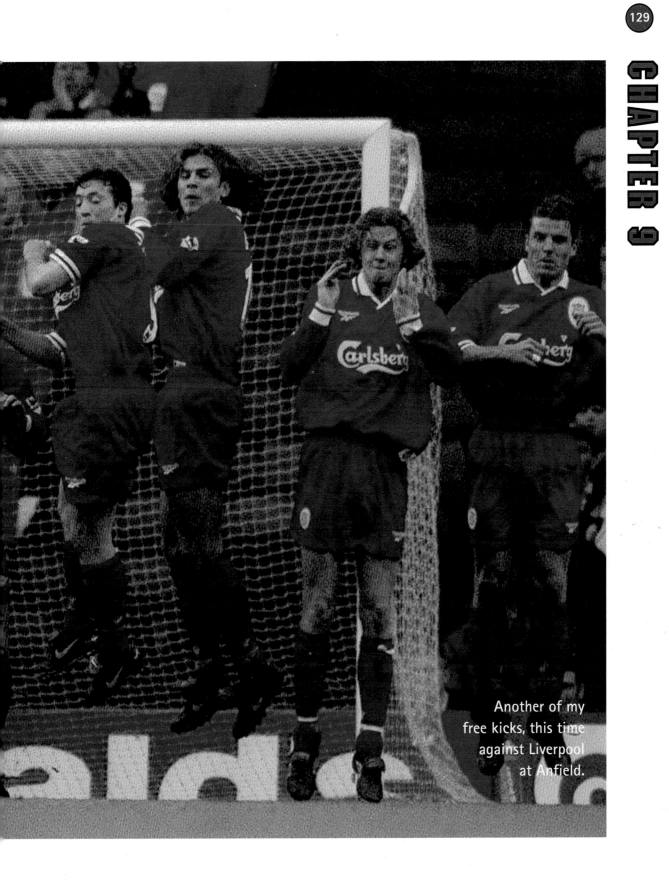

Another of my
free kicks, this time
against Liverpool
at Anfield.

Champions' League when everyone thought Liverpool would make it. I wondered what Kevin Keegan was thinking.

What is it that makes a championship side? An inner belief in what you are doing, a tremendous team spirit, leadership you can trust, the knowledge that no one individual is bigger than the club, a sense of belonging and an absolute faith in each other. We have that at Manchester United, fostered partly by so many of us having come through the youth team together. But every player at United, whether they've been at the club from the start of their careers, or brought in from elsewhere, understand what being at this club really means.

It is a privilege few people are able to enjoy. I am one of the fortunate ones, and I'm going to keep on giving it everything I can. I know I am expected to improve year on year, that is what being a United player demands of you and I'm ready for that challenge.

I'm still learning the game. I know what people expect of me, because I expect nothing less of myself.

That is what being a professional footballer is all about. It is certainly what being a Manchester United player is about.

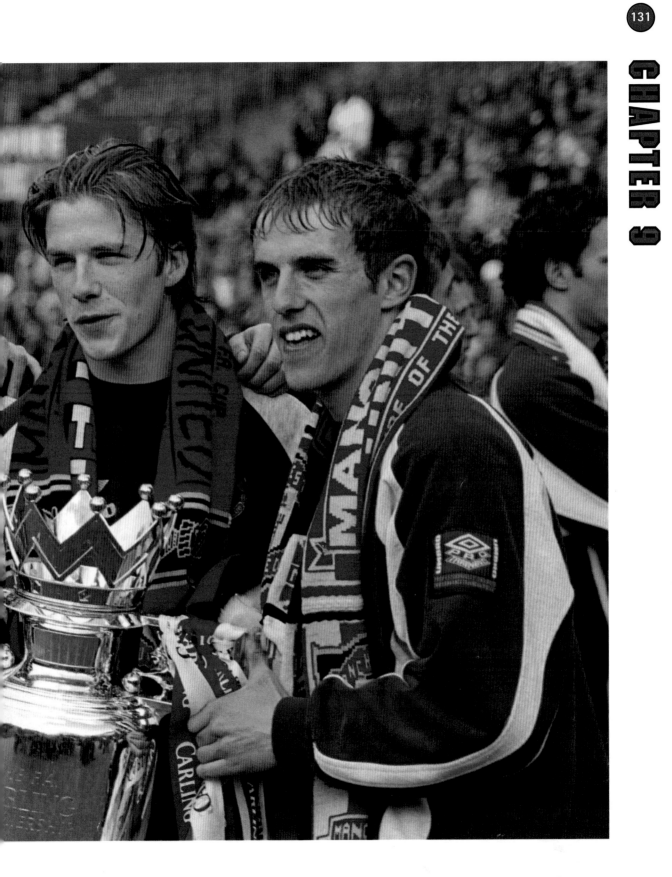

Poland v. England

31 MAY 1997

For once, England came to Manchester to prepare for the World Cup qualifier in Poland that was to have such a crucial bearing on our chances. A game against South Africa had been arranged for Old Trafford, the chance for northerners, who have a great passion for their country, to see the England team on their own doorstep. We prepared at Mottram Hall, which is every bit as superb as Burnham Beeches. I would have liked to play in the game but I was one of the subs. There was a terrific atmosphere, and we won the match 2-1, but there was a cost. I can't believe how unlucky Jamie Redknapp has been with injuries playing for England. He was stretchered off in the first half, when he'd been playing so well and then, in the final minute, Gazza was taken off on a stretcher, too. Maybe, Old Trafford was going to curse us, and there were only seven days left to prepare for Poland.

We were based right out in the wilds, well away from the town of Katowice, to try to keep us focused for the game. They don't come much more important. Gazza was fit for the game, but he didn't last more than about 20 minutes. By then, though, we were a goal up, a quite brilliant pass by Incey splitting the Polish defence. Alan was onto it like a shot and finished absolutely superbly. The first part of the plan worked, because we wanted to try to unnerve the Poles, to give them a fright.

Then we got a penalty in the last minute of the half. Alan was held down, quite clearly, but you don't always get those kind of decisions away from home. We thought the game would be wrapped up, but Alan hit the post. A couple of seconds later the whistle went for half-time. We went in with mixed emotions.

England 2 (Shearer, Sheringham) Poland 0

Poland: Wozniak, Zielinski, Jozwiak, Kaluzny, Ledwun, Bukalski (Swierczewski), Nowak (Kucharski), Waldoch, Majak, Dembinski, Juskowiak (Adamcyzk).

England: Seaman, G, Neville, Campbell, Ince, Southgate, Le Saux, Beckham (P Neville), Gascoigne (Batty), Shearer, Sheringham, Lee.

ATTENDANCE: 32,000.

Glenn put us right back on track, though. We had to forget the penalty, it was old news. We had done half of a terrific job, and now it was time for us to show our real mettle. I thought we were brilliant in the second half – I don't think Gary Neville has ever played so well; Sol and Gareth Southgate were solid as rocks and in the last minute Rob Lee went through half their defence, rounded the keeper and unselfishly laid the ball off for Teddy to finish the game. We went wild. Three away games, three wins, no goals conceded, a terrific record. And now we were right back on track.

Le Tournoi
4 JUNE TO 10 JUNE.

I suppose you could say this was a bitter-sweet experience for me. So much happened in such a short space of time, it was hard to take it all in. We were based near Nantes, in the north-west of France, in a superb facility. There was a lot of talk among the boys that this was where we would be stationed if we qualified for the World Cup, which was something to look forward to. The first game was against Italy, our old World Cup foes, in Nantes itself. Paul Scholes, who had come on as a sub against South Africa, was given his debut, and no one deserved it more. I got the chance to play in the centre of midfield and I have to say, it was a game I enjoyed as much as any other the entire season. I felt as fresh as I had ever been. United were the champions, England had won in Poland and here I was, in against Italy with a new responsibility. I loved it. There was only Paolo Maldini missing from the side which had done us over at Wembley, so they were taking it seriously, no doubt about it. I thought we were brilliant.

Scholesy set up the first with one of the most brilliant passes of the season. I could see what he was trying to do from the moment he got possession, and the ball sat up brilliantly for Ian Wright to score from the edge of the area. A couple of minutes before half-time, Wrighty sped down the left and crossed for Scholesy to finish with a great left-footed volley. The Italian coach, Cesare Maldini, Paolo Maldini's dad, said he would see us in Rome, but we knew he had an even greater respect for us now.

Proud to be representing my country as always.

I was delighted with the way that I had played, but I got myself booked for standing up for Gary Neville and arguing with the referee when he should have penalised the Italians for a terrible foul on Gary. Once again, some of the Press tried to make out I was getting a temper, but I

that's being played now at such a pace. I'd be out there in the middle waving my arms all over the place, not knowing what I was doing. I've got a grudging respect for referees, though I know there are certain people out there who think that Manchester United are a team who moan at them and try

At full stretch . . . limbering up before the match against Italy.

felt Gary hadn't been protected properly. I suppose I let my feelings for a mate cloud my better judgement. Something to learn from, and not just for England games.

Being a referee is something I just couldn't do, to have to make instant judgements on a game

to influence them. I'd like to think you could ask anyone who's refereed me, and they would say I was a fair player. I can say categorically that I have never tried to intimidate a referee and I don't believe anyone at Manchester United has, either. I think there is something in the

Sometimes, this international football takes some working out.

It's the will to win that we have. We aren't offensive towards referees. I have been booked for dissent a couple of times, but that's been more through over-exuberance than because of malicious back-chat. If you let your concentration wander by having a go at the ref, you're not going to be at your best when you need to be. It is a message Alex Ferguson constantly gets across to us – don't get involved in things you can't do anything about. Let the referee make his decisions and accept them the best you can.

Three days after Italy, we flew down to Montpellier to play France, the hosts. We had won our last five games under Glenn and the adrenalin was really pumping. We won the game through a typical poacher's goal from Alan Shearer in the last couple of minutes, but people seemed to be more interested in the fact that I'd been booked for not getting onto a stretcher after a tackle by

argument that referees are a little bit intimidated by coming to Old Trafford, it's such a fantastic place to play your football and it must be a pretty daunting place to have to come and control a match involving United. The pressure is definitely on. They must get nervous about walking

out there in front of over 50,000 people, but I suppose it's like it is for us, a great shot of adrenalin. Yes, we get hyped up before matches, we want to win them, and if decisions don't go your way, it's difficult sometimes to hide the fact that you're not happy. It's all part of the game.

Arsenal's Patrick Vieira. I was moving into the French half when I was suddenly sent spinning into the air. I didn't think much of the tackle, I'll leave it at that. Gary Lewin, the physio came on. I was hobbling, but I didn't see the need to get onto the stretcher as I could limp off. The referee was from Morocco and didn't understand what we were trying to say. I was still incensed with the challenge when suddenly he had shown me the yellow card. I was devastated as it meant I would miss the match against Brazil.

It was another lesson to learn with the World Cup a year ahead. You do what the referees tell you to do, even if you feel aggrieved. I had to sit out the final game, which we lost 1-0, and I was desperately down on myself. The Brazilians were great to watch, scoring a wonderful goal through Romario, but I just wanted to be out there. Games against Brazil might come along once in a lifetime and, because of a reaction I regretted in the cold light of day, I'd let myself and the team down. Glenn made certain, by taking me through the situation on video in front of the whole squad when we were preparing for the Moldova match, that I knew where I stood. The lads didn't make too much of it, but I was told I couldn't argue with referees at this level.

We won Le Tournoi, despite defeat by Brazil. It was a perfect end to a perfect season. United were champions, and England were back on course for the World Cup. What young footballer could want for more?

We win Le Tournoi. Now for the biggest prize of all . . .

LE TOURNOI –

Italy 0 England 2
4 June 1997 Nantes.

Italy: Perruzi, Ferrara (Nesta), Costacurta, Cannavaro, Di Livio (Mannini), D Baggio, Albertini, Di Matteo (Fuser), Benarrivo, Zola, Casiraghi.
England: Flowers, P Neville, Pearce, Keown, Southgate, Le Saux (G Neville), Beckham, Ince, Wright (Cole), Sheringham (Gascoigne), Scholes.
ATTENDANCE: 30,000.

France 0 England 1
7 June 1997 Montpellier.

France: Barthez, Blanc, N'Garry, Largle, Thuram, Vieira, Deschamps, Keller, Djorkaeff, Dugarry (Zidane), Ouedec (Loko).
England: Seaman, G Neville, Campbell, P Neville, Southgate, Le Saux, Beckham (Lee), Gascoigne, Shearer, Wright (Sheringham), Batty (Ince).
ATTENDANCE: 25,000.

Brazil 1 England 0
10 June 1997 Paris.

Brazil: Taffarel, Celio Silva, Dunga, Aldair, Cafu, Flavio, Denilson (Djalminha), Roberto Carlos, Leonardo (Ze Ruberio), Romario, Ronaldo.
England: Seaman, Keown (G Neville), Campbell, Ince, Southgate, Le Saux, P Neville, Gascoigne, Shearer, Sheringham (Wright), Scholes (Lee).
ATTENDANCE: 50,000.

Other results:
France 1 Brazil 1 (Lyon)
Brazil 3 Italy 3 (Lyon)
France 2 Italy 2 (Paris)

England win the trophy.

England win the trophy

England v. Moldova

10 SEPTEMBER 1997

I never had the chance to meet Princess Diana, and I would loved to have done so just once. There are already many nights in my career that I will never forget, but Wednesday 10 September at Wembley will remain one of the most vivid. It was the most unbelievable occasion.

Footballers are no different from anyone else. I too was absolutely devastated when the Princess of Wales was killed, it all seemed so senseless. No one knew quite what to say to each other, we all just walked around with sad faces. Two days after her death, the England squad for the Moldova game was announced and I remember chatting with Gary Neville, saying that if we were lucky enough to play and the game went ahead, it would be one of the most incredible nights of our life. We knew there would have to be some sort of tribute, because it was going to be the first gathering of people for a sporting occasion since the day of the funeral.

The preparation for the game wasn't any different from the usual, apart from the fact that when we weren't on the training field, we didn't seem to be talking much about football. Usually, it's the only thing we're interested in. The mood was subdued, but we knew we had a match to win, and that the nation would be with us like never before.

When we drove up to Wembley there was none of the usual cheering and waving. I knew this was going to be difficult. Glenn had told us beforehand that even he didn't know what to expect, that we had to deal with the inevitable emotions in our own way and then try to get on with the job as professionally as we could in the circumstances.

We were just coming out of the dressing room when the 'Candle in the Wind' song was being played. To hear 80,000 people singing it was almost too much for us to take in. Then, as we came out, instead of flags, there were candles everywhere. I don't think I've ever known such

---

England 4 (Scholes, Wright 2, Gascoigne) Moldova 0

England: Seaman, G Neville, Southgate, Campbell, Beckham (Ripley, replaced by Butt), Batty, Gascoigne, P Neville, Scholes, Ferdinand (Collymore), Wright.

Moldova: Romanencu, Secu, Sirasco, Testimitanu, Eginu, Shishkin, Curtean, Culibaba, Rebeja, Mitereu, Clescenco.

ATTENDANCE: 74,102.

emotion. I looked across at the Moldova side and their faces seemed to be pretty blank. If we couldn't comprehend it all, what must they have been thinking?

The Moldovan national anthem was sung with the utmost respect, then after a marvellous rendition of ours, there was the one minute's silence. It was only right and proper. I remember looking down, closing my eyes for a time, then staring at the turf. There wasn't a breath of noise. I could feel my heart pounding. Then the roar broke across the pitch. I knew we would win. We had to.

We seemed to win so many corners in the early stages of the match, I spent the first 15 minutes running from one corner flag to the other. It wasn't much of a surprise to me that we should eventually score from one of them; their goalkeeper punched out one of my inswingers from the left and I decided to send it back in, first time. There was Scholesy, darting in between their defenders, to head home. The Manchester United connection had worked for England again and we felt much more settled.

We scored almost immediately after half-time, when Gazza picked the ball up on the halfway line, and sent three defenders spinning out of his path, before sliding a pass through to Ian Wright, on his left foot. Wrighty struck it perfectly. The manager decided I had done my share, though I didn't much like being taken off, but it had been a night of such emotions, I had probably run further and done more than I needed to, purely on adrenalin. I was delighted that Stuart Ripley, who had an outstanding start to the season with Blackburn, should get his chance, and mortified when he pulled a hamstring only eight minutes after coming on. Poor Stuart seemed to be fated when he played for England, his only other appearance had been in San Marino, when we were already out of the 1994 World Cup.

We did score a couple more, Gazza producing a peach of a goal and then Wrighty completing the job in the final minute. The team was very proud of the job it had done in unique circumstances. We just hoped we would never have to go through such emotions again. This was a tribute to Princess Diana, and the remarkable effect she had had on the nation came home to us all that night.

UMBRO

Italy v. England
11 OCTOBER 1997

Another one of those occasions you will never forget. I have to say that my first thought was that the England players would be more nervous than they were, but there was the same kind of determination and inner belief that we've grown to expect at Old Trafford. We knew how much hype and publicity there would be surrounding the game and it was important we didn't get caught up in the whole thing. We were shielded

from any exposure to the English papers – we didn't want anything to interfere with our preparations. It was, after all, the biggest game some of us had ever been involved in, myself included.

Before the squad left for Rome, there had been stories that Glenn was thinking of leaving me out for tactical reasons, and I suppose, yes, I was worried that I wouldn't play. I wanted to be out there, that was the end of it. Glenn never mentioned to me that he had ever considered not playing me.

There was a calming-down stage when everything began to fit into place for us. The

One of the most shattering and uplifting nights of my life, against Italy in The Stadio Olimpico.

players were very relaxed going into the game, but then I shouldn't have been too surprised, what with the likes of Tony Adams, Paul Ince, David Seaman and Paul Gascoigne who have seen and been through so much in their careers in the team. Glenn Hoddle was really relaxed. I had gone into the training session the night before the game when the Press were there, with a really heavy cold and I had to pull out before the end of the evening, because I was having trouble breathing properly. Of course, many questions were being asked and I suppose I was a bit worried because no one can ever be complacent about their place in an England team, and this was such an important match, that anyone who was less than 100 per cent couldn't have been risked.

If other players in the team thought we might have been carrying someone, they'd get tense themselves. I was passed fit that night, as it

happens, but I don't think the manager told anyone else but me that I was definitely playing. It's amazing how you can feel better so quickly! I have to say that the team were perfectly prepared, we all knew what was at stake, and nothing had been left to chance. We knew what we had to do, we knew our functions in the team, and we played it just about as perfectly as we could have done in the circumstances. Glenn has never been the sort of manager to stop me going forward if I thought there was a chance of exploiting any weakness in the opposition, but he said to me that night, 'Be careful', and, 'You've got to keep the ball, don't give it away'. The night before the game I had one of my worst night's sleep ever. Then the day itself was the longest of my life because I was so looking forward to the game. I just wanted to get out there. In the morning, we were up in time for breakfast at about ten o'clock, then out for a walk, and then it was back to the rooms for a sleep in the afternoon. Amazingly, I slept like a baby then.

Soon it was time to get ready for the game. It took us about an hour to get to the Olympic Stadium, and a pretty interesting hour it was, riding in the coach through the throng of Italian supporters. I don't know exactly what they were chanting at us, but I don't think it left much to the imagination. When we got to the stadium, most of the fans seemed to be inside already and when we came out at the start each and every one of the Italians raised little cardboard squares in their national colours. It was an amazing sight. Having said that, I'd rather play in front of 100,000 people against me than 10,000 for me, so the atmosphere didn't bother me at all. The more the merrier.

The match itself? I have to confess that Maldini, a great player, was giving me a lot of trouble early on. Zola was coming over on to our right side as well, Maldini was getting around the back and it seemed as if I had both of them bombing at me. It wasn't easy at that stage. In truth, it was never easy. Then Maldini got an injury and had to go off, midway

It wasn't an easy match: Zola and Maldini gave me lots of trouble early on.

through the half. I was pretty pleased to see him go, I have to say. I'm sure Glenn would have swapped things around, but once Maldini was off, the pressure was never as bad again. Then, of course, I had that chance. It was a great build-up, probably our best move of the night. When Teddy knocked the ball back into my path, I had only one thought in my mind. I was certain I was going to score. I decided to hit the ball first time, but I caught it with the outside of my foot rather than the instep and it sailed just wide of the far post. I ran my hands through my hair, looking in disbelief at where the ball finished up. It wasn't that far away. (Don't ask me how I would have celebrated that goal, I don't think anyone would have ever stopped me to find out). But I had wasted the chance to seal our place in the World Cup Finals. Would that one come back to haunt me? It was important to try to get it out of my mind as quickly as I could.

The guys were unbelievable that night. Paul Ince's performance was superhuman. He went off after a nasty clash of heads and came back on with a huge bandage swathing the injury, but the blood was still seeping through. I remember some years ago seeing a picture of Terry Butcher with his England shirt stained in blood but a look of utter determination in his eyes. A bit frightening really. Incey was the same and he galvanised me. Gazza was having a brilliant game as well – the Italians were trying to upset him but he didn't rise to the bait, he just kept concentrating on his football, and also on lifting the players around him. The last minute of the match was something else. I was caught in some kind of trance when Wrighty went through, and round the goalkeeper, Peruzzi. Here it was, the

World Cup at his feet, we were through. Then the ball came back off the post and I must admit my legs froze a bit as the ball bounced back down the Italian left. I swear I wasn't supposed to have been marking the guy who crossed from my side, I was just coming back across the half way line when the ball floated across our penalty area. All I remember is feeling as though my heart was going to come out of my chest, it was pounding that much. I could see Christian Vieri rising for it. I really thought it was in as from where I was standing there seemed no way he could miss. I was nearly on my hands and knees crying. Incredibly, he missed it. I was so relieved, it's hard to describe it. When the whistle went a minute or so later – it was a minute I was told later although it had seemed like five or ten out there – I didn't know what to do next. Gary was first to me as usual – me and my best pal were going to the World Cup and we were delirious with excitement. I raced around. I remember hugging Incey and Gazza. What heroes they had been! I think I was dragged in front of the cameras by Sky TV, but I don't remember what I said, I just hope it made some kind of sense because my mind was going round and round, dizzy with delight. Back in the dressing room everyone was on such a high. The World Cup Finals, what an achievement.

Italy 0   England 0

Italy: Peruzzi, Nesta, P Maldini (Benarrivo), Albertini, Cannavaro, Costacurta, Di Livio, D Baggio, Vieri, Zola (Del Piero), Inzaghi (Chiesa).

England: Seaman, Campbell, Le Saux, Ince, Adams, Southgate, Beckham, Gascoigne (Butt), Wright, Sheringham, Batty.

ATTENDANCE: 81,200.

The elation was incredible, but we were also exhausted. We just sat there for a while, thinking through the game and also the implications. Everything just caught up with us. I had never experienced anything like that as a player before. The nearest I had come to it was the FA Cup Final against Liverpool in 1996 when Eric Cantona scored the winner so close to the end of the game. We had had a lot to prove that day, we were going for the double, they wanted the trophy. That was one of the best games I'd had for United. I was really involved and I almost scored in the first five minutes. I had kept the ball well throughout, and we scored the only goal of the game from my corner. I think I was the first to Eric as he ran to the United supporters kissing his shirt. I don't know how I had the energy to leap onto his back, but I did.

That was the most excited I had been after a game, probably because it was the first time I had played at Wembley, representing the club of my dreams. All my family were there, we had won the final, and I had contributed a large part, I felt, to our success. The FA Cup Final is very special. To have all those people out there, in the national stadium, cheering for you, is almost indescribable. But if that was the most exciting, then Rome was most satisfying professionally – and the most exhausting.

Someone asked me later whether I realised I was the only player who had started in every one of Glenn's World Cup sides and it got me thinking what a fantastic achievement it was for me and my family. All those hours of work, all the journeys up to Manchester, all the encouragement and support, everything had fallen into place. I was very thankful that I had the talent to have been involved in such a great journey with the England team and with Glenn, one of my playing heroes. It's still hard to take in that a man I so admired should be picking me on such a regular basis for England and placing such faith in me. Unbelievable (my favourite word, as if you hadn't noticed).

Reputat

I love being a professional footballer. From the moment I first kicked a ball I never wanted to be anything else. Now there are times when my life isn't my own, and that scares me a bit. I know I am a high-profile player in the highest-profile club of them all and, because of my talents, I get the opportunity to play for my country. Those opportunities excite me and, ultimately, are my reason for being. With all of this, of course, comes the attention, some of it nice, some not so nice.

People start to think they can say what they like about you. It seems to me that as you come through the youth ranks and become regarded as a potential first teamer, everyone wants to praise your abilities, to write about how far you might be able to go in the world and to marvel at your potential. A young lad's head can be turned by all of this adulation unless he has a family who have brought him up

ion

My Dad's having a special room built for all my trophies.
I treasure them all.

Meeting the Prince of Wales at Wembley. I suppose it's only right that Giggsy should be next to him.

properly and he works with people who teach him how he should behave.

Manchester United must be the finest teacher in the world, bar none. Once you break through into the first team – if you're one of the lucky ones – the Press gets more and more interested in every facet of your life – what you do, where you go, what you eat, who you go out with, what you drive, where you live. It can become suffocating if you let it. I know there have to be critics, it is the same in all walks of life. If you want to be a professional footballer, you must realise there are people out there who will praise you and others who will look to accentuate the negative. People will begin to tag you with a reputation, but it's largely something they want you to be rather than how you really are. I would be lying if I didn't say that at times this season certain things have been creeping in to other people's perceptions of me which have hurt, and hurt a lot.

Against the Dutch side Feyenoord in the Champions' League at Old Trafford, I made a tackle on one of their players which, I admitted straight after the game, was unintentional. I would never go over the top against any player on purpose. I had gone into the challenge just trying to win the ball and had landed on his ankle, but there was no intent to hurt him. All of a sudden, people start saying that I'm getting too big for my boots and that I'm a nasty so-and-so on the field. It goes to amazing extremes. One writer – who I don't think even watches Manchester United live more than a couple of times a season – says that I'm going to be more

At a charity event with Steve Coogan.

trouble to Alex Ferguson than George Best was to Matt Busby. What gives people the right to make wild assumptions like that? Ask Alex Ferguson if I'm any trouble to him. People close to me know what sort of person I am, outsiders don't. The article in question was written on the day we played Tottenham at Old Trafford. My Dad was really upset by it and,

to be honest, it got to me as well. I don't like people saying I'm getting too big for my boots. I had a very quiet game that day. I shouldn't really blame any outside influences, but it was one of my least productive performances for United, even though both goals came from my crosses. Some of the lads had read the piece and they said it was just typical of the way so many newspapers have gone downhill these days. I know I have a lot to live up to and that if I don't play well from the word go, it's noticed by people.

I'm conscious of the demands on me. I want to carry on and learn as much as I can. It gets a little bit tedious when everyone has a view on me, when the cameras are pointing at me all the time. I've said all along that I know it's part and parcel of the game, but it does seem as though some people are just there to try and catch you out.

Against Chelsea in the FA Cup third round tie in January, although I was really up for the game, I had a pretty poor first half until I scored the opening goal. I actually looked at my feet after 15 minutes to make sure I'd put my boots on the right way round. I set my own standards. I want to live up to them, to match them, and to better them if I can. The manager has his standards as well, and we have to live up to those. But there are other people who think we should live up to their standards, without ever having the nerve to say things to your face. I suppose I should try to ignore what's written about me, but when it starts to affect your family, it's hard to cut yourself off from the criticism.

I've got a girlfriend in the public eye and unfortunately the Press seem to think it's more interesting to have pictures of, for example, Victoria and me walking our dogs than it is to write about matters which are of real importance. I've got to live with the fact that there's nothing I can do about any of this, but it does make you wonder.

At times, I can see why people want to pack it all in and get out of the country when the hounding becomes intolerable. I'm too young at the moment to think of anything like that. I love my football, I love Manchester United and I want to be a part of this club for a long time to come. But at the same time I can see how

people would choose a more normal life. It has become so intense.

On Christmas Day, the Press were outside the house, waiting for Victoria and me. Haven't these people got family to go to? Am I that important? The mind boggles. We wanted to have a quiet family Christmas and we weren't allowed to. The cameras seemed to be everywhere. But, I do go out sometimes. In January, I was invited, through Manchester United, to go to Milan to see a Versace clothes show, and I said I wanted to go. Even though it was a day off, I checked with the manager that it wasn't going to affect any of my responsibilities for the club. If it

They say football is an art!

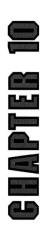

had, I wouldn't have gone, simple as that. There's no way I would let anything get in the way of my professional life. I respect Manchester United too much for that. But, needless to say, I ended up on the front pages again with fictitious stories about me planning to become a Versace model!

I have made a point of insisting that I don't want to be involved with anything that interferes with my football. It is being a footballer that's given me these opportunities and I'm not about to waste the chance I've been given. That would give the Press the right to have a go at me, and then I couldn't complain.

It's unbelievable for me even to think that some people could consider me a superstar. I could never have dreamt of it – young kids when asked who their favourite player is, saying 'David Beckham'. It only seems five minutes ago I was playing for Ridgeway Rovers. It does me in when I see young lads walking down the street with my shirt on. Although I wore Bryan Robson's shirt and Glenn Hoddle's shirt, it's hard to think that I've come so far that kids are saying they want to be just like me. To be honest, it's a little nerve-racking. I know there are people out there who admire me as a footballer, and that is the one and only thing that matters. Of course, I'd like to be known as a good bloke, someone who never let anyone down, who behaved properly, who did right by people, who treated other people the way he liked to be treated himself, but it's football that has got me where I am today, and it's my life.

At the Versace show in Milan. That side of things is fun but I would never let anything get in the way of my professional life.

It is those who want to talk to me about football – not the other things that have or haven't happened to me – that interest me. I have always taken the time to sign autographs for as many people as I can. It's the way I was brought up. My dad has always drummed it into me to be polite, to say hello, to speak to people, because ultimately they are the ones who pay your wages, and they are the ones who will either make or break you. There was an suggestion in the 'Too Big for his Boots' piece that I'd offended a certain well-known rugby player because I'd deliberately turned my back and refused to sign his autograph. I'd like to have known who he was, because if it's true, and I can't believe it is, I'd like to have the chance to apologise to him. I would never, ever ignore someone who asks me politely for an autograph.

Epilogue

There are so many people to thank who have helped me during my career so far, and if I've left anybody out, I hope they won't be too offended. My Mum, my Dad, my nan, grandad and my sister, have never stopped supporting me and have always been there when I needed encouragement. There's my youth team manager Stuart Underwood and Steve Kirby, one of my dad's friends who helped with my training as a youngster. There's Malcolm Fidgeon, Manchester United's London-based scout, who started my career off with the club. I'll always be enormously thankful to him, for having faith, for seeing my potential and for getting me to Manchester and back so many times. Gary Peters at Preston changed my whole career around, thanks Gary.

Eric Harrison, the greatest youth team coach in the country, taught me all the right things, and took time to encourage me when things weren't always going well. Brian Kidd has been a great influence, someone who knows what it's like to be a successful Manchester United player, coming from

Manchester himself and steeped in the club. And, of course, there's the manager. As I've said before, he scares me stiff, but from the moment I gave him that pen when I was 12 years old, I've never looked back. It's been a fantastic ten years for him at Manchester United and a terrific eight for me since I signed as a schoolboy. Glenn Hoddle had the faith in me to give me a chance with England and let me go out and express myself. His first game as England coach was my first as an England player, so we'll always have that to remember. It is quite amazing that someone you idolised as a kid should have such an influence on you. It must have taken a lot of courage for him to go with me against Moldova, a World Cup qualifier on an away ground. I hope I've lived up to his expectations and that we can help England to World Cup glory one day.

There are just so many people to thank. If I've left
anyone out, hopefully they're in this picture!

Afterword by
Alessandro

I have met David Beckham and I like him. He is a fine person and, of course, a very fine footballer as well.

The football in England has a lot to be pleased about as we in Italy have found to our cost in recent months and one of those things is the emergence of so many young players who have the talent to take the step from their club to European and international football. The best tribute I can pay to David is that he has graduated with no fears, he does not look out of place, he is a true international.

The progress of the English national team, from the time we beat them in the World Cup qualifier at Wembley last year, has impressed us all. When they came to Rome last October, they only needed a draw to win the group and they achieved that with a superb performance. We had to applaud them for the strength of their character and especially that of their younger players. The atmosphere that night could have turned them cold, but they played through it superbly.

David Beckham is one of the young inspirations. Manchester United have played Juventus in the last two seasons in the Champions' League

Del Piero

and they have improved so much from the first time we met them, they are now considered in Italy as one of the most influential sides in Europe.

I am a forward and there is a great thrill in that, but it can also bring an enormous pressure because people expect you to perform all the time, there is little consideration given if you drop below your best. It is not easy to live up to the expectations of others.

I have seen David Beckham score some spectacular goals. He is one of those players who excites a crowd, who brings them to the height of their emotions. It is the joy of football to make people happy by expressing your talent, it is what makes me happy and it is what makes David happy too.

The chance to express these few words on David's behalf gives me great pleasure, because I know he is going to be a very fine player for many seasons to come. Who knows, one day he might come to Italy, where I know he would have the talents to succeed. That might not be good news in Manchester, but I know from speaking to him that he loves his club very much. That is very important these days.

It is right that England have qualified for the World Cup. I know how much it has meant to the people here that the Italian team, the Azzurri, has reached France, '98.

I wish David Beckham every success in the rest of his career. I would say to him never to forget how important football is. Football is the greatest game in the world, it gave him the chance to fulfil his dreams. He has a great talent and he must not waste it. There are not many second chances in football – he must live for the day and not for tomorrow.

David, my friend, take care and good luck.

Alessandro Del Piero. Juventus FC, February 1998.

Facts

1994–95 Season

7 (4) appearances

1 goal

1995–96 Season

32 (7) appearances

8 goals

1996–97 Season

45 (3) appearances

11 goals

1997–98 Season (up to the end March 1998)

39 (4) appearances

8 goals

Picture Acknowledgments

Front cover: Moy Williams

Back cover: Moy Williams left, NTI top, Action Images centre, Colorsport bottom

Jacket flap: Frank Spooner Pictures

Action Images 26-27, 36, 56, 57 left, 58, 62-63, 72-73, 77 top, 104, 116, 127, 130-131, 136, 141, 144-145; Action Plus 34-35, 96 bottom; Action Plus/Glyn Kirk 123, 124, 134; Action Plus/Neil Tingle 31 bottom, 91, 131; Allsport/ Shaun Botterill 70, 156; Allsport/Clive Brunskill 114; Allsport/Phil Cole 88; Allsport/David Cannon 60, 61; Allsport/Stu Forster 120; Allsport/Ross Kinnaird 28, 30, 31 top, 90; Allsport/Ben Radford 140, 142; Allsport/ David Rogers 37; Allsport/Mark Thompson 6, 98; Allsport/Hulton Deutsch 64, 65 bottom; Big Pictures 44, 45, 49, 152, 153; Colorsport 22, 32, 65 top, 71, 85, 89, 94, 100-101, 109, 119, 125, 135; Empics 86-87; Empics/Matthew Ashton 86-87, 105; Empics/Steve Etherington 96 top; Empics/Laurence Griffith 57 right, 111; Empics/Tony Marshall 81; Empics/Neal Simpson 92, 93, 113; Empics/Michael Steele 95, 97; Empics/Chris Turvey 147 top; Express Newspapers 8, 11 top, 14, 17, 18, 33, 51, 79, 106-107, 128-129, 148-149; Frank Spooner Pictures 2, 50, 74, 84; Lancashire Evening Post 39; The Mail on Sunday 69; Manchester Evening News 66; Mirror Syndication International 42, 43, 46, 47, 54, 55, 103, 151; Newsquest (North London) 15, 16; News Team Manchester 25; PA News Photo Library 147 bottom; Paul Docherty International 76-77; John Peters 20, 21, 23, 24; Sporting Pictures (UK) Ltd 8, 29; Waltham Forest Gazette 10, 11 bottom, 12, 13; Moy Williams 3, 41, 53, 80, 102, 122, 139.

Images taken from the Beckham family scrapbook 10, 11, 19, 66 146, 155.

The author and publishers have made every reasonable effort to contact all copyright holders. Any errors or omissions are inadvertent and anyone who for any reason has not been contacted is invited to write to the publisher so that a full acknowledgement may be made in subsequent editions of this work.

OTHER TITLES AVAILABLE FROM MANCHESTER UNITED BOOKS

0 223 99178 6	*Manchester United in the Sixties* by Graham McColl	£12.99
0 233 99340 1	*Manchester United: The Insider's Guide*	£9.99
0 233 99359 2	*Sir Matt Busby: A Tribute* by Rick Glanvill	£14.99
0 233 99359 2	*Cantona on Cantona* by Eric Cantona	£14.99
0 233 99047 X	*Alex Ferguson: Ten Glorious Years*	£9.99
0 233 99368 1	*A Will to Win: The Manager's Diary* by Alex Ferguson with David Meek	£6.99
0 233 99362 2	*Odd Man Out: A Player's Diary* by Brian McClair with Joyce Woolridge	£6.99
0 233 99417 3	*The Official Manchester United Quiz Book*	£9.99

All these books are available from your local bookshop or can be ordered direct from the publisher.

THIS SEASON'S VIDEOS FROM VCI

MUV27	*Champions Again! Season's Review 96/97*	£13.99
MUV28	*Alex Ferguson's Ultimate United*	£13.99
MUV29	*David Beckham – Football Superstar*	£13.99
MUV 32	*Au Revoir Cantona*	£10.99
MUV33	*300 Manchester United Premiership Goals*	£10.99
MUVM5001	*Manchester United On Video Vol. 5 No. 1*	£ 7.99
MUVM5002	*Manchester United On Video Vol. 5 No. 2*	£ 7.99
MUVM5003	*Manchester United On Video Vol. 5 No. 3*	£ 7.99
MUVM5004	*Manchester United On Video Vol. 5 No. 4*	£ 7.99